REFORMATORY SCHOOL, HAZARIBAGH AND PRESENT JUVENILES

DR. BUDHADEV MISHRA

1

Dedicated to my parents, and my father who served from 1926 to 1959.

3

Preface

Child of a social community of a specific nation represents future of the country on human values , talents and ability of that civilization. In present world we need culture of world as one family and one home with happiness and peace. With present day Modern society having conflicts and mistrust between various sections, class, groups and country, we should make effort to rebuild our children to think of noble society. Proper guidance and training is necessary for children from family up to the country. We must try not to ignore juvenile child from proper training and education to lead a valued life style. Government or rulers have responsibility for them. Reformatory school under an act should be properly understood in our country where government has accountability for delinquents. Mere legislation being a part of present democracy system should not thrust the task of reforming juvenile delinquents on private organisations

This book may help policy makers to take proper ways to reform and rehabilitate juvenile delinquents of our country.

-Author

<u>Preface</u>
<u>Content</u>

1. Reformatory School Act, Hazaribagh, Infrastructure

Same certificate must have been notified in present world philosopher say that child is the father of the man. Shaping of childhood though vests with family but various factors make a child to be harmful in social orders. If child base is not restructured at primitive stage, there is option of many to obtain unwise path in a society. They become unruly and antisocial indulging themselves in wrong path and criminal actions. Present day world with conflicts, aspirations, polluted environment, mechanical activities, unlimited wants, easy contacts with another world, manly considerations of a better social life are gradually shrinking. Culture and tradition have little influence for a better society.

For a better human its upbringing from birth to youth stage is very significant. This is gradually shrinking for modernization and adoption of western culture. Simultaneously it is affecting entire world due to bad culture and present days surroundings. weaponization, terrorism,

aspirations of highlife style, lack of spiritual faith, commercial education, illiteracy, intolerance, lack of adjustment etc. are major

6

factors of growth of child criminality. Family being smaller with one or two child concentrates with extraneous passion of guardians towards children. There is gradual increasing trend of criminal activities of children in India along with other country. Though Britishers had realized this part of problem and did not find any data in India on child delinquents but they took steps to check the child delinquency first time in India in 1876 through a frame work of regulation.

In 1853, Charles Hathaway, inspector general of Punjabi memo to the provincial government of India first one mentioned problems of juvenile offenders. As per him till then there was no system on punishment of child criminals in India's also mentioned reform of juveniles observing 400 child criminals in jail every year there. In madras presidency by 1890, 700 juveniles per year were convicted. Similar trend was seen in eastern India particularly from west Bengal. Many cases of similar nature of child conviction were seen from Maharashtra in Bombay. More cases became conspicuous in then cities now recognized as metros. Britishers realized its concerns and brought Reformatory act as preventive measure.

Britishers adopted Reformatory act 1897 initiated from 1876 and prescribed all means of education to child convicts starting from skill developments up to class room study the act is placed below.

Central Government Act

The Reformatory Schools Act, 1897

THE REFORMATORY SCHOOLS ACT, 1897

ACT NO. 8 OF 1897 1 [11th March, 1897.]

An Act to amend the law relating to Reformatory Schools and to make further provisions for dealing with youthful offenders.

Whereas it is expedient to amend the law relating to Reformatory Schools and to make further provision for dealing with youthful offenders; It is hereby enacted as follows:-

1. Title and extent.

(1) This Act may be called the Reformatory Schools Act, 1897 2

(3) 3 It extends to the whole of India except 4 the territories which, immediately before the 1st

November, 1956, were comprised in Part B States].] 2 a Repeals. 2 and 3. [Repeals.] Rep. by

the Repealing Act, 1938 (1 of 1938), s. 2 and Sch.

4. Definitions. In this Act, unless there is anything repugnant in the subject or context, -

(a) 5; youthful offender; means any boy who has been convicted of any offence punishable

with transportation or imprisonment and who, at the time of such conviction, was under the age

of fifteen years:

(b) " Inspector General" includes any officer appointed by the State Government to perform all

or any of the duties imposed by this Act on the Inspector General: and

1. Rep. in W. Bengal by W. Bengal 30 of 1959.

1. The provisions of this Act, except s. 15, cease to be in force in the areas where the Madras

Children Act, 1920 (Mad. 4 of 1920), or the Bengal Children Act, 1922 (Ben. 2 of 1922), is in

force.

2. The word" and" and sub-section (2) rep. by Act 10 of 1914, s. 3 and Sch. II.

3. Subs. by the A. O. 1948, for the original sub- section (3) as amended by the A. O. 1937.

4. Subs. by the Adaptation of Laws (No. 2) Order, 1956, for" Part B States".

5. In Bombay the age- limit has been raised to 16; see the Bombay Children Act, 1924 (Bom. 13

of 1924), s. 4. In the C. P. this definition has been replaced by another; see the C. P. children

Act, 1928 (C. P. Act 10 of 1928), s. 3. Extended to the whole of Madhya Pradesh by Madhya

Pradesh Act 23 of 1958 (When notified).

(c) " District Magistrate" shall include a Chief Presidency Magistrate. II.-REFORMATORY SCHOOLS

5. Power to establish and discontinue reformatory schools. 1 The State Government may-

(a) establish and maintain Reformatory Schools at such places as it may think fit;

(b) use as Reformatory Schools schools kept by persons willing to act in conformity with such

rules, consistent with this Act, as the State Government may prescribe in this behalf;

(c) direct that any school so established or used shall cease to exist as a Reformatory School or to

be used as such.

6. Requisites of Schools. Every school so established or used must 'provide-

(a) sufficient means of separating the inmates at night;

(b) proper sanitary arrangements, water-supply, food, clothing and bedding for the youthful

offenders detained therein;

(c) the means of giving such youthful offenders industrial training;

(d) an infirmary or proper place for the reception of such youthful offenders when sick.

7. Inspection of Reformatory Schools.

(1) Every school intended to be established or used as a Reformatory School shall, before being

used as such, be inspected by the Inspector General, and if he finds that the requirements of

section 6 have been complied with, and that, in his opinion, such school is fitted for the reception

of such youthful offenders as may be sent there under this Act, he shall certify to that effect, and such certificate 2 shall be published in the Official Gazette, together with an order of the State

Government establishing the school as a Reformatory School or directing that it shall be used as

such, and the school shall thereupon be deemed to be a Reformatory School.

(2) Every such school shall, from time to time, and at least once in every year, be visited by the

said Inspector General, who shall

1. The words" With the previous sanction of the G. G. in C." rep. by Act 4 of 1914, s. 2 and Sch.,

Pt. I.

2. For instance of the publication of such a certificate, see C. P. R. and O.

send to the State Government a report on the condition of the school in such form as the State

Government may prescribe.

8. Power to Courts to direct youthful offenders to be sent to Reformatory Schools.

(1) Whenever any youthful offender is sentenced to transportation or imprisonment, and is, in the

judgment of the Court by Co which he is sentenced, a proper person to be an inmate of a

Reformatory School, the Court may, subject to any rules made by the State Government, direct

that, instead of undergoing his sentence, he shall be sent to such a school, and be there detained

11

for a period which shall be not less than 1 three or more than seven years.

(2) The powers so conferred on the Court by this section shall be exercised only by (a) the High

Court, (b) a Court of Session, (c) a District Magistrate, and (d) any Magistrate specially

empowered by the State Government in this behalf, and may be exercised by such Courts

whether the case comes before them originally or on appeal.

(3) The State Government may make rules for-

(a) 2 defining what youthful offenders should be sent to Re- formatory Schools, having regard to

the nature of their offences or other considerations, and

(b) regulating the periods for which youthful offenders may be sent to such schools according to

their ages or other con- siderations. 3

9. Procedure where Magistrate is not empowered to pass an order under section 8.

(1) When any Magistrate not empowered to pass an order under the last foregoing section is of

opinion that a youthful offender convicted by him is a proper person to be an inmate of a

Reformatory School, he may, without passing sentence, record such opinion and submit his

proceedings and forward the youthful offender to the District Magistrate to whom he is

12

subordinate.

(2) The Magistrate to whom the proceedings are so submitted may make such further inquiry (if

any) as he may think fit and pass such sentence and order for the detention in a Reformatory

School of the youthful offender, or otherwise, as he might have passed if such youthful offender

had been originally tried by him.

1. This part of the section has been amended in Bombay by the Bombay Children Act, 1924

(Bom. 13 of 1924), s. 4, and in the C. P. by the C. P. Children Act, 1928 (C. P. 10 of 1928), s. 3.

2. For rules made under this clause by the Punjab Government, see Punjab Gazette,

Extraordinary, dated 2nd October. 1903, p. 3.

3. For rules regulating the period for which youthful offenders may be sent to Reformatories, see

different local R. and O.

10. Power of Magistrates to direct boys under fifteen sentenced to imprisonment to be sent to

Reformatory Schools. The officer in charge of a prison in which a youthful offender is confined,

in execution of a sentence of imprisonment, may bring him, if he has not then attained the age of

fifteen years, before the District Magistrate within whose jurisdiction such prison is situate; and such Magistrate may, if such youthful offender appears to be a proper person to be an inmate of a

Reformatory School, direct that, instead of undergoing the residue of his sentence, he shall be

sent to a Reformatory School, and there detained for a period which shall be subject to the same

limitations as are prescribed by or under section 8, with reference to the period of detention

thereby authorised.

11. Preliminary inquiry and finding as to age of youthful offender.

(1) Before directing any youthful offender to be sent to a Reformatory School under section 8,

section 9 or section 10, the Court or Magistrate shall inquire into the question of his age and,

after taking such evidence (if any) as may be deemed necessary, shall record a finding thereon,

stating his age as nearly as may be.

(2) A similar inquiry shall be made and finding recorded by every Magistrate not empowered to

pass an order under section 8 before submitting his proceedings and forwarding the youthful

offender to the District Magistrate as required by section 9, sub- section (1),

14

12. Government to determine Reformatory School to which such offenders shall be sent. Every

youthful offender directed by a Court or Magistrate to be sent to a Reformatory School shall be

sent to such Reformatory School as the State Government may, by general or special order,

appoint for the reception of youthful offenders so dealt with by such Court or Magistrate:

Provided that, if accommodation in a Reformatory School is not immediately available for such

youthful offender, he may be detained in the juvenile ward or such other suitable part of a prison

as the State Government may direct-

(a) until he can be sent to a Reformatory School, or

(b) until the term of his original sentence expires, whichever event may first happen. Should the

term of his original sentence first expire, he shall thereupon be released, but, should he be sent to

a Reformatory School, then the period of detention previously undergone shall be treated as

detention in a Reformatory School.

13. Persons found to be over eighteen years not to be detained in Reformatory School.

15

(1) If at any time after a youthful offender has been sent to a Reformatory School it appears to

the Committee of Visitors or Board of Management, as the case may be, that the age of such

youthful

offender has been understated in the order for detention, and that he will attain the age of

eighteen years before the expiration of the period for which he has been ordered to be detained,

they shall report the case for the orders of the State Government.

(2) No person shall be detained in a Reformatory School after he has been found by the State

Government to have attained the age of eighteen years.

14. Discharge or removal by order of Government. The State Government may at any time order

any youthful offender-

(a) to be discharged from a Reformatory School;

(b) to be removed from one Reformatory School to another such school situate within the

territories subject to such Government:
Provided that the whole period of his detention in a

Reformatory School shall not be increased by such removal.

16

15. 1 Agreement between States. The State Governments of any two States may after mutual
agreement, generally or specially, notify in their respective Official Gazettes that any
Reformatory School situated in one of the States shall be available for the reception of youthful
offenders directed to be sent to a Reformatory School by any Court or Magistrate in the other
State and may thereupon make provision for the removal of youthful offenders accordingly.]

16. Certain orders not subject to appeal or revision. Nothing contained in the 2 Code of Criminal
Procedure, 1882 (10 of 1882), shall be construed to authorise any Court or Magistrate to alter or
reverse in appeal or revision any order passed with respect to the age of a youthful offender or
the substitution of an order for detention in a Reformatory School for transportation or
imprisonment. III.- MANAGEMENT OF REFORMATORY SCHOOLS

17. Appointment of Superintendent and Committee of Visitors or Board of Management.

(1) For the control and management of every Reformatory School, the State Government
shall 3 appoint either (a) a Superintendent and a Committee of Visitors, or (b) a Board of
Management.

1. Subs. by the A. O. 1937, for the original s. 15.

2. See now the Code of Criminal Procedure, 1898 (5 of 1898).

3. For notification making such appointments, see different local Rules an Orders.

(2) Every Committee and every Board so appointed must consist of not less than five persons 1 .

(3) The State Government may suspend or remove any Super intendent or any Member of a

Committee or Board so appointed.

18. Superintendent may license youthful offenders to employers of labour.

(1) Every Superintendent so appointed may, with the sanction of the Committee, by license

under his hand, permit any youthful offender sent to a Reformatory School, who has attained the

age of fourteen years, to live under the charge of any trustworthy an respectable person named in

the license, or any officer of Government or of a Municipality, being an employer of labour and

willing to receive and take charge of him, on the condition that the employer shall keep such

youthful offender employed at some trade, occupation or calling.

(2) The license shall be in force for three months and no longer but may, at any time and from
time to time until the expiration of the period for which the youthful offender has been directed
to be detained, be renewed for three months at a time.

19. Cancellation of license. The license shall be cancelled at the desire of the employer named in
the license.

20. Determination of license. If during the term of the license the employer named therein dies,
or ceases from business or to employ labour, or the period for which the youthful offender has
been directed to be detained in the Reformatory School expires, the license shall thereupon cease
and determine.

21. Cancellation of license in case of ill-treatment. If it appears to the Superintendent that the
employer has illtreated the youthful offender, or has not adequately provided for his lodging and
maintenance, the Superintendent may cancel the license.

22. Superintendent to be deemed guardian of youthful offenders.

19

(1) The Superintendent of a Reformatory School shall be deemed to be the guardian of every

youthful offender detained in such school, within the meaning of 2 Act No. 19 of 1850

(concerning the binding of apprentices).

(2) Power to apprentice youthful offender. If it appears to the Superintendent that any youthful

offender licensed under section 18 has behaved well during one or more periods

1. The words" of whom two at least shall be Natives of India omitted by the A. O. 1950.

2. The Apprentices Act, 1850.

of his license, the Superintendent may, with the sanction of the Com- mittee, apprentice him

under the provisions of the said Act, and on such apprenticement the right to detain such

youthful offender in a Reformatory School shall cease and the unexpired term (if any) of his

sentence shall be cancelled.

23. Duties of Committee of Visitors.

(1) Every Committee of Visitors appointed under section 17 for a Reformatory School shall. at

least once in every month,--

(a) visit the school, to hear complaints and see that the requirements of section 6 have been

complied with, and that the at management of the school is proper in all respects

(b) examine the punishment- book;

20

(c) bring any special cases to the notice of the Inspector- General; and

(d) see that no person is illegally detained in the school.

(2) If any member of a Committee of Visitors so appointed fails or neglects, during a period of

six consecutive months, to visit the school and assist in the discharge of the duties aforesaid, he

shall cease to be a member of such Committee.

24. Powers of Board of management. If, in exercise of the power conferred by section 17, the

State Government appoints a Board of Management for any Reformatory School, such Board

shall have the powers and perform the functions of the Superintendent under sections 18 to 22,

both inclusive; an the license mentioned in section 18 may be under the hand of their chairman;

and they shall be deemed to be the guardians of the youthful offenders detained in such school.

25. power to appoint trustees or other managers of a school to be a Board of Management. The

State Government may declare any body of trustees or managers of a school, who are willing to act in conformity with the rules referred to in section 5, clause (b), to be a Board of Management

under this Act, and thereupon such body or manager shall have all the powers and perform all the

functions of such Board of Management.

26. Power of Board to make rules.

(1) With the previous sanction of the State Government, every Board of Management of a

Reformatory School may from time to time make rules consistent with this Act-

(i) to prescribe the articles which are to be deemed to be" prohibited articles"; and

(ii) to regulate-

(a) the conduct of business of the Board; (b) the management of the school; (c) the education and

industrial training of youthful offenders;

(d) visits to, and communication with, youthful offenders;

(e) the terms and conditions under which any articles declared by the Board to be" prohibited

articles" may be introduced into or removed out of the school;

(f) the manner in which such articles are to be removed when introduced without due authority;

(g) the conditions and limitations under which such articles may be supplied outside the school to any youthful offender under order of detention therein;

(h) the conditions on which the possession by any such youthful offender of such articles may be

sanctioned;

(i) the penalties to be imposed for the supply or pos- session of such articles when supplied or

possessed without due authority;

(j) the punishment of offences committed by youthful offenders; and

(k) the granting of licenses for the employment of youthful offenders.

(2) In the absence of a Board of Management the State Government may make rules consistent

with this Act to regulate for any Reformatory School the matters mentioned in any clause of sub-

section (1), other than clause (ii) a, and also the mode in which the Committee of Visitors shall

conduct their business. IV.- OFFENCES IN RELATION TO REFORMATORY SCHOOLS

27. Penalty for introduction or removal or supply of prohibited articles and communication with

youthful offenders. Whoever, contrary to any rule made under section 26, introduces or removes

or attempts by any means whatever to introduce or remove into or from any Reformatory School, or supplies or attempts to supply outside the limits of any Reformatory School to any youthful

offender under order of detention therein, any prohibited article,

and every officer or person in charge of a Reformatory School who, contrary to any such rule,

knowingly suffers any such article to be introduced into or removed from any Reformatory

School, to be possessed by any youthful offender detained therein, or to be supplied to any such

youthful offender outside its limits, and whoever, contrary to any such rule, communicates or

attempts to communicate with any such youthful offender, and whoever abets any offence made

punishable under this section, shall, on conviction before a Magistrate, be liable to imprisonment

for a term not exceeding six months, or to fine not exceeding two hundred rupees, or to both.

28. Penalty for abetting escape of youthful offender. Whoever abets an escape, or an attempt to

escape, on the part. of a youthful offender from a Reformatory School, or from the employer of

such youthful offender, shall be punishable
with imprisonment for a term which may extend
to

six months, or with fine not exceeding two
hundred rupees, or with both.

29. Arrest of escaped youthful offender. A
Police- officer may, without orders from a
Magistrate

and without a warrant, arrest any youthful
offender sent to a Reformatory School under this
Act,

who has escaped from such school or from
his employer, and take him back to such school
or to

his employer. V.- MISCELLANEOUS

30. [Application of Act 15 of 1869 to
youthful offenders detained in Reformatory
Schools.] Rep.

by the Prisons Act, 1900 (3 of 1900), s. 53
and Sch. III.

31. Power to deal in other ways with youthful
offenders, includind girls.

(1) Notwithstanding anything contained in
this Act or in any other enactment for the time
being

in force, any Court may, if it shall think fit,
instead of sentencing any youthful offender to

transportation or imprisonment or directing
him to be detained in a Reformatory School,
order

him to be-

(a) discharged after due admonition, or

(b) delivered to his parent or to his guardian or nearest adult relative, on such parent, guardian or

relative executing a bond, with or without sureties, as the Court may require, to be responsible

for the good behaviors of the youthful offender for any period not exceeding twelve months.

(2) For the purposes of this section the term " youthful offender shall include a girl.

(3) The powers conferred on the Court by this section shall be exercised only by Courts

empowered by or under section 8.

(4) When any youthful offender is convicted by a Court not empowered to act under this section

and the Court is of opinion that the powers conferred by this section should be exercised in

respect of such youthful offender, it may record such opinion and submit the proceedings and

forward the youthful offender to the District Magistrate to whom such Court is subordinate.

(5) The District Magistrate to whom the proceedings are so sub- mitted may thereupon make

such order or pass such sentence as he might have made or passed if the case had originally been

tried by him.

32. Procedure when youthful offender under detention in a Reformatory School is again

convicted and sentenced. When a youthful offender during his period of detention in a

Reformatory School is again convicted by a Criminal Court, the sentence of such Court shall

commence at once, notwithstanding anything to the contrary in section 397 of the 1 Code of

Criminal Procedure, 1882 (10 of 1882), but the Court shall forthwith report the matter to the

State Government, which shall have power to deal with the matter in any way in which it thinks

fit,

1. The relevant provisions of the Code of Criminal Procedure, 1898 (5 of 1898) may now be

referred to.

S

Prior to coming of British in India the action of the children were governed under Hindu and

Muslim law in which concerned family was monitoring action .Some law between 1850 to 1919

came in British India like apprentice act 1850, code of criminal procedure act 1861, Reformatory

school act 1876- 1897.Under apprentice act 1850 pretty offenders between age of 10 to 18 years

on conviction were to work as apprentices for businessman. under Indian penal act 1860, the

27

children between 7 to 12 years were accountable for punishment. Code od criminal procedure act

1861 allowed prosecution of children under age 15 under reformatory values or reformation

.rather than prisons. It provided probation of young offenders. Such action showed change in

attitude and approach of juvenile delinquents and change from penal to reformation .There fore

Reformatory school act 1876 and 1897 was harbinger of such legislation. Under the act, the

delinquents were put in the Reformatory school for a period of 2 to 7 years. On attending the age

of 18 they were put to adult prison .Treatment and rehabilitation of young offenders was dealt in

1897 act.It was an act which benefitted many convicted juveniles who after completion of term

having background of vocational education there were able to earn through employment.

Prior to that the apprentices which was passed on 11 th april 1850 had a provision of vocational

training during imprisonment. There was no separate institution for the child convicted tbe

brought under reformation the apprentice act 1850 is reproduced below All these proposal and

actions of britishers originate from report
communication from Charles Hathway,
Inspector
General of prisons, Punjab 1853 in a memo
to the provincial government . In his mention
about
problems of juvenile offenders he pointed for
juvenile reforms as 400 children every year in
Punjab are passing through jail life.. he
suggested for law by the government as no
information
on records of data was available. In madras
presidency about 700 juveniles per year were
convicted and put to jails. In significant
proportion juveniles from west Bengal and
maharastra
were also put to prisons which should have
been given scope of children as they were
minors and
had tremendous scope of leading a good life
other than criminal scope .All the juveniles were
being treated by criminal procedure act 1861
existing then .British government then started to
make laws for children with apprentices
training background and started institutions
providing
base structures for reformation purpose. By
the period there was considerable improvements
in
the implementation of reform policy . The
apprentice law 1860 is given belowr

29

It may be recalled that efforts were made by the British government all along to take care of rehabilitation of individuals who might have done offence also as child because he must have to be given scope of earning for whole of the life after release. Then government there fore thought to bring apprentice act in India, Now the principle though is same being replaced as Act 1961 but the application is in pen and paper only. Application of this law now needs to be understood by the readers, so that a comparative facts can be drawn for the understanding of the common man in the country

We shall like to reproduce initial base of clauses adopted in 1850 in our country. While presenting the clauses which are very old in nation, but are still useful law for the juveniles

I.—LABOUR.

ရ။ ။အလုပ်သမားဆိုင်ရာ။

THE APPRENTICES ACT.

[INDIA ACT XIX, 1850.] (11th April, 1850.)

Preamble.

For better enabling children, and especially orphans and poor children brought up by public charity, to learn trades, crafts and employments, by which, when they come to full age, they may gain a livelihood ; It is enacted as follows :—

Apprenticing of child between ten and eighteen years.

1. Any child, above the age of ten and under the age of eighteen years, may be bound apprentice by his or her father or guardian to learn any fit trade, craft or employment, for such term as is set forth in the contract of apprenticeship, not exceeding seven years, so that it be not prolonged beyond the time when such child be of the full age of twenty-one years, or in the case of a female, beyond the time of her marriage.

Evidence of age in questions as to right to service.

2. The age set forth in the contracts shall be evidence of the age of the child, in all questions which arise as to the right of the master to the continuance of the service.

Powers of Magistrate acting for orphans, etc.

3. Any Magistrate may act with all the powers of a guardian under the Act, on behalf of any orphan, or poor child abandoned by its parents, or of any child convicted before him or any other Magistrate of vagrancy, or the comission of any petty offence.

Apprenticing of child brought up by public charity.

[1] 4. An orphan or poor child, brought up by any public charity, may be bound apprentice by the governors, directors or managers thereof, as his or her guardians for this purpose.

5—7. *   *   *   *

Form and contents of contract of apprenticeship.

8. Every contract of apprenticeship shall be in writing, according to the form given in the Schedule (A) annexed to this Act, or to the like effect, which shall set forth the conditions agreed upon, particularly specifying the age of the apprentice, the term for which he is bound, and what he is to be taught.

Signatures to contract.

9. Every such contract shall be signed by the person to whom the apprentice is bound, and by the person by whom he is bound, and by the apprentice, when he is of the age of fourteen years or more at the time of binding : but when the apprentice is bound by the governors, directors or

---

[1] Instruments of apprenticeship executed by a Magistrate under this Act or by which a person is apprenticed by or at the charge of a public charity are exempted from stamp duty [see Art. 9, Schedule I of the Burma Stamp Act].

managers of a public charity, the signature of two of them, or of their secretary or officer shall be sufficient on behalf of the persons binding the apprentice.

10. No such contract shall be valid unless it be executed in the manner aforesaid, nor until it has been deposited in the office of the District Magistrate of the place or district where it has been executed, and the person in whose office any such contract is deposited shall give to each of the parties a copy thereof, certified under his hand. Contract not valid unless executed as prescribed and deposited. Copies to be given to parties.

11. The terms of service may be changed at any time during the apprenticeship, or the contract may be determined, with the consent of both parties to the contract or their personal representatives, and with the consent of the apprentice if he is above the age of fourteen years : Provided that the changes agreed to or the termination of the contract shall be expressed in writing on the original contract, with the signature of the proper parties according to section 9 of this Act ; and the Magistrate shall thereupon make under his hand corresponding endorsements on the office copies, which shall be brought to him at the same time for that purpose. Alteration of terms of service and termination of contract.

12. The master of any apprentice bound under this Act may, with the consent of the person by whom he was bound, and with the consent of the apprentice if he is above the age of fourteen years, assign such apprentice to any other person, who is willing to take him for the residue of his apprenticeship, and subject to the conditions thereof : Provided that such person shall, by endorsement under his own hand on the contract, declare his acceptance of such apprentice, and acknowledge himself bound by the agreements and covenants therein mentioned, to be performed on the part of the master, and that the consent of the other parties aforesaid shall be expressed in writing on the same, and signed by them respectively : And every such assignment shall be certified on the office copies of the contract under the hand of the Magistrate according to the form given in Schedule (B) annexed to this Act. Assignment of apprentice to new master.

13. Upon complaint made to any Magistrate, by or on behalf of any apprentice bound under this Act, of refusal or neglect to provide for him, or to teach him according to the contract of apprenticeship, or of cruelty, or other ill-treatment by his master, or by the agent under whom he shall have been placed by his master, the Magistrate may summon the master or his agent, as the case may be, if he shall be within his jurisdiction, to appear before him at a reasonable time, to be stated in the summons, to answer the complaint ; Powers of Magistrate in case of complaint by apprentice against master.

and at such time, whether the master or his agent be present or not (service of the summons being proved), may examine into the matter of the complaint ; and, upon proof thereof, may cancel the contract of apprenticeship, and assess upon the offender, whether he shall be the master or his agent, a reasonable sum for behoof of the apprentice, not exceeding four times the amount of the premium paid upon the binding, or if no premium or a less premium than fifty rupees was paid, not exceeding two hundred rupees ;

and, if the offender shall not pay the sum so assessed, may levy the same by distress and sale of his goods and chattels, and, if the offender shall not be the master but his agent, by distress and sale of the goods and chattels of the master also.

Powers of
master or his
agent to
chastise
apprentice.

Liability of
master or
agent for
assault, etc.

14. No contract of apprenticeship shall be cancelled, nor shall any master or his agent be liable to any criminal proceeding, on account of such moderate chastisement for misbehaviour, given to any apprentice by his master or the agent of his master, as may lawfully be given by a father to his child ; and the provision for enabling the contract of apprenticeship to be cancelled shall not bar any criminal proceeding against any master or his agent for an assault or other offence committed against his apprentice, for which he would be liable to be punished had it been against his child, whether or not any proceedings be taken for cancelling the contract of apprenticeship.

Power of
Magistrate
in case of
complaint
by master
against
apprentice.

15. Upon complaint made to any Magistrate, by or on behalf of the master of any apprentice bound to him under this Act, of any ill-behaviour of such apprentice, or if such apprentice shall have absconded, the Magistrate may issue his warrant for apprehending such apprentice, and may hear and determine the complaint, and punish the offender by an order for keeping the offender, if a boy, in confinement in any debtor's prison or other suitable place, not being a criminal gaol, for any time not exceeding one month, of which one week may be in solitary confinement, during which time such allowance shall be made for his subsistence by the master or his agent as the Magistrate shall order : and, if the offender be a boy of not more than fourteen years of age, may order him to be privately whipped : or, if the offender be a girl, or in the case of any boy, the Magistrate deem any such punishment unfit, he may pass an order empowering the master of the apprentice or his agent to keep the offender in close confinement in his own house, or on board the vessel to which he belongs upon bread and water, or such other plain food as may ·be given without injury to the health of the apprentice, for a period not exceeding one month.

Cancelment
of contract
for miscon-
duct of
apprentice.

16. Upon complaint of wilful and repeated ill-behaviour on the part of the apprentice, and on the demand of the master, the Magistrate may order the contract of apprenticeship to be cancelled, whether or not the charge is proved ; but only with the consent of the apprentice and of his father or guardian, if the charge is not proved : and such cancelling shall be with or without refund of the whole or part of any premium that may have been paid to the master on binding such apprentice, as to the Magistrate seems fit on consideration of the case ; and all sums so refunded shall be applied under the direction of the Magistrate for behoof of the apprentice.

17. The Magistrate may order any sum recovered for behoof of the apprentice on cancelling the contract to be either laid out in binding him to another master, or otherwise for his benefit, or to be paid to the person by whom any premium was paid when he was bound apprentice.

Appropriation of sum recovered for apprentice on cancelment of contract.

18. No Magistrate shall entertain a complaint on the part of a master against an apprentice under this Act unless it be brought within one month after the cause of complaint arose, or, if the cause of complaint arose on board ship during a voyage, within one month after the arrival thereof at a port or place in the Union of Burma : and no Magistrate shall entertain a complaint on the part of an apprentice against his master or the agent of his master under this Act unless it be brought within three months after the cause of complaint arose, or, if the cause of complaint arose on board ship during a voyage, within three months after the arrival thereof at a port or place in the Union of Burma.

Limitation of complaint of master against apprentice : of apprentice against master s.

19. If the master of any apprentice shall die before the end of the apprenticeship the contract of apprenticeship shall be thereby determined ; and a proportionate part, corresponding to the unexpired portion of the term, of any premium which shall have been paid to such master on the binding of the apprentice to him shall be returned by the executors or administrators out of the estate of the deceased to the person or persons who shall have paid the same ; unless the executors or administrators of the deceased master shall continue the business in which such apprentice shall have been employed, and shall, within three months from the death of the late master, make offer in writing to keep the apprentice on the terms of the original contract ; in which case the estate of the deceased shall be discharged from all liabilities on account of such premium.

Effect of death of master during apprenticeship.

Offer by representatives of deceased master to continue to keep apprentice.

20. If such offer to keep the apprentice shall be made as aforesaid, the same shall be fully expressed and certified by the executors or administrators on the original contract of apprenticeship, and also on the office copies thereof, by the Magistrate, and the apprentice shall be bound to the executors or administrators so keeping him for the remaining term of his apprenticeship.

Offer to be certified on original contract and copies.

21. Any apprentice bound under this Act, whose master shall die during the apprenticeship, shall be entitled to maintenance for three months from and after the death of his master out of the assets left by him : Provided that during such three months such apprentice shall continue to live with, and serve as an apprentice, the executors or administrators of such master, or such person as they appoint.

Maintenance of apprentice whose master dies.

Apprentice to continue to serve.

22. The apprentice of any person against whom a commission of bankruptcy shall be issued, or who shall be adjudged to have committed an act of insolvency, during the apprenticeship, shall be discharged from all obligation under the contract of apprenticeship : and, if any premium was

Effect of insolvency of master during apprenticeship.

paid on binding him as an apprentice, he or a person by whom he was bound shall be entitled to claim the amount thereof as a debt against the estate of the bankrupt or insolvent.

23. *   *   *   *

Appeal from orders of Magistrates.

24. An appeal shall lie from any order passed by any Magistrate to the Court of Session to which such Magistrate is subordinate, provided the appeal is made within one month from the date of the order.

Interpretation of terms.

25. In this Act, the words " master ", " owner ", "person ", and the pronoun " he " shall be understood to include several persons as well as one person, and females as well as males, and bodies corporate as well as individuals, unless there is something in the context repugnant to such construction.

SCHEDULE A.

FORM OF AGREEMENT.

THIS AGREEMENT made the   day of   in the year   between *A.B.*, of   , and *C.D.*, of   witnesseth that the said *A.B.* doth this day bind *E.F.*, a boy (or girl) of the age of   years completed, son (or daughter) of the said *A.B.* (or otherwise describing the relation in which *A.B.* and *E.F.* stand), to dwell with and serve the said *C.D.*, as an apprentice, from this day forth for   years (in the case of a girl add, or until the time of her marriage, which shall first happen), during all which term the said apprentice shall duly and faithfully serve the said *C.D.*, according to his (or her) skill and ability in all lawful business, and demean and behave himself (or herself) honestly, orderly and obediently, in all things, towards the said *C.D.* and his (or her) family. And the said *C.D.* for himself (or herself) and his (or her) executors and administrators, in consideration [of the premium or sum of   paid by the said *A.B.* to the said *C.D.*, the receipt whereof the said *C.D.* hereby acknowledges, and] of the faithful

If there is no premium the words between brackets may be omitted.

service of the said *E.F.*, doth covenant and agree with the said *A.B.*, his (or her) executors and administrators, that he (or she) will teach or cause to be taught to the said *E.F.*, in the best way and manner that he (or she) can, the trade (craft or employment) of a   during the said term ; and will also, during the said term, find and allow unto the said apprentice good, wholesome and sufficient food, clothes, lodging, washing, and all other things necessary, fit and reasonable for an apprentice : (and further, *here insert any special covenants*).

In witness whereof the parties have hereunto set their hands the day and year above written.

A.B.

C.D.

SCHEDULE B.

Form of Order of Assignment.

(To be endorsed on the Agreement.)

Be it Known to all men that on the day of   in the year   personally appeared before *G.H.*, Magistrate of   , *C.D.*, of   with *E.F.*, his (or her) apprentice and *I.K.*, of   , and desired that the agreement of apprenticeship whereby the said *E. F.* was bound to the said *C.D.* might be assigned and made over to the said *I.K.*, and the said *G.H.*, having satisfied himself, by personal examination of the said *E.F.* and by other lawful ways and means, that such assignment is for the benefit of the said *E.F.*, and is made with the consent of [the said *E.F.*, and of] all persons whose consent thereunto by law is required, doth allow such assignment; and the contract of apprenticeship whereby the said *E.F.* was on the   day of   in the year

If E.F is not above the age of fourteen years, the words between brackets may be omitted.

bound to the said *C.D.* as an apprentice to learn the trade (craft or employment) of a   shall henceforth endure, unto the end of the said term, as if the said *I.K.* had been originally party to the said deed, and had executed the same, in the place and stead of the said *C.D.*, and shall be bound, for himself (or herself), his (or her) executors or administrators, to fulfil the covenants by the said *C.D.* to be performed, and the said *E.F.* shall henceforth be bound unto the said *I.K.*, in like manner as he (or she) was by the said agreement bound unto the said *C.D.*

C.D.   E.F.   I.K.

In witness whereof the said *C.D.*, *E.F.* and *I.K.* have hereunto set their hands before me the day and year above written.

G.H.
Magistrate.

Closed workshop photographs installed then with foreign equipment now seen as wasted one due to closure of the Reformatory school, Hazaribagh.

It may be noted that various divisions in the work shop was being operated in lower portion of the various dormitories having sufficient light and open air space installed with usable instruments for giving training to the inmates as well as learners in Diploma institute and Industrial Training Institute.

Photo graph of the Birmingham machine from England in entry passage amid two big gates.

Weighing machine from Birmingham, London.as explained above .This machine was being used then for materials inside by truck or other importing system to bring perfection im measurement for purchase and payments.

The entry system being common for staffs and inmates , there was tough scrutiny system before entry doors .There fore above weighing machine was installed as shown in above figure.

Golghar attached to dormitory no.2 shown in above photo which was connected with dormitories.

Accordingly britishers framed regulation of the Reformatory school act 1897 keeping apprentice

act 1860 in mind. under paragraph 5 of the Reformatory act state government was allowed to

maintain, establish Reformatory schools. There were essential requisites condition. Requisite

school must provide sufficient means to
separate inmates in night hours, proper sanitary
arrangements, water supply, food , clothing,
bedding for youth offenders. This also had a
condition of having sufficient means of
giving an infirmary or proper place or hospital
for
reception of such youthful offenders when
sick.
Under clause 6 there was provision that
Inspector general should inspect every year the
place and
certify that all the requisites condition are
completed.. The same certificate must have to be
notified every year in official gazette and
state government must notify the place to be
used as
Reformatory school. As per agreement vide
clause 15 two states should mutually agree to
notify
in their respective gazette that Reformatory
school situated in one of the state shall be
available
for the reception of the youth ful offender
decided to be sent to the Reformatory school by
any
cort or magistrate in other state and there
upon make provisionfor release of youthful
offender
accordingly.

41

In back ground of the law Hazaribagh
happened to be most favourable choice because
of
location, geography, climate and
infrastructure complying both the act of 1860
and
1897.Available structure of gora jail meant
for foreigners in india conviction got recognition
as
Reformatory school in eastern india having
convicted by the courts from Bihar, west Bengal,
Assam and Odisha. During that period Assam
was a big state which now is bifurcated as
Manipur, Mizoram, Meghalaya etc.The
campus of the school is near then central jail of
Hazaribagh established for adults where
freedom fighters like jayprakash narayan etc
were
kept.The pattern of buildings, enclosures,
staff quarters, farming campus, pattern of
building
with locations of superintendant and officers
are more or less similar. Reformatory school
superintendant quarter in one side of lake is
seen with quarter of the jail superintendant.
Other
side of the lakes Pattern of deputy
superintendant of Reformatory school is similar
to jailor of the
central jail .Reformatory school had better
infra structure and beauty for frontal play ground

42

,lakes, plantations etc It is said that before operation of the Reformatory school at hazaribagh the

building and infrastructures were kept for british soldiers. However Britishers were sending

grown up freedom fighters in forest of hazaribagh where they were captured by wild animals in

deep forest. But authentic records are not available to substantiate the views.Britishers were

keeping eye on youths agitating against their rule.The infrastructure of this school was unique.

The design was a british reformator jail with school, workshops, gymnasium , dormitories, play

ground, hospitalfull of water facility electrical facility, good sanitation , long high brick walls

attached to warden quarter, doctor quarter, hybrid cow sheds and beautiful to look at. The walls

had security staffs with gun at gumbaj at corners where watch was being made to protect

inmates.The entry was two big gate systems for entry of staff instructors of the workshops and

others who were allowed to enter after verification in gates having small enteries.The supply of food materials in truck were being weighed in measuring system brought from burminghum,

England instead of measuring in small slots brought in trucks by the suppliers to the institution

against payments. The bigger suppliers under rules were from Hazaribagh town traders. From the

town the suppliers in major proportion were Mahabir Prasad jain, Inder lal jain and others who

used to supply in bulks by trucks and materials were being weighed along with trucks.

The entry gate was placed in two parts. Each part had smack gate for entry of individual either

on duty or on visit. Two gates were only allowed for supply components in truck which was

being weighed by measuring machine brought from England as stated above. Staffs were

deployed 24 hours for entry screenings of the persons coming for duty and boys going outside

for fatms, play ground, cattle farm duty etc. In addition the staffs of Diploma poly technics and

students wee being allowed to go to workshop. The students admitted under Industerial training

institute and trainees of Teachers training centre were being allowed to enter through gates for workshop. The Diploma institute was giving 3 years training certificate in mechanical

engineering where as 1 year certificate course was being given by I. T. I.. In teachers training

centre teachers from Bihar government were being deputed for short course refresher training.

All institutions were provided hostels.Ram rekha singh was in charge of diploma centre. The

management of three institution establishes infrastructure quality of Reformatory school

constructed by the britishers which was training spot for the employments of inmates after

reformation.

Big workshop of foreign machines with different trades was a remarkable gift of british

government for training of inmates.Vrious trades in lower floor of three big dormitories were

operating as workshops. There was a big store with stocks of Burma teak woods and other parts.

T he trades were fitter, welder, carpenter, weaving, sewing, book binding,colouring and

painting,motor mechanic,electrical,mechanical, and other trades. The instructors were from

Hazaribagh town mainly who used to com on duty in 1 st hour and return by 2 o clock as second half was fixed for inmates in school teaching programme.Nagen Chandra roy was foreman.Sri ram singh was Assistant foreman staying in residential colony.The infra structure was so bigger

that government had started 3 year diploma course for out siders and students passing from there were being employed in other places .After training they were trained and experienced and

worked at steel plants and other industries. industrial training institute and teachers training

centre ..with closure of institution, costly machines were dumped to gather and locked as wasted

. The photographs is given.

Names of the staffs in workshop

Nagen ch. Roy , Foreman .
Sriram singh Asst
Foreman
INSTRUCTORS

Kartik Prasad motor mechanic section.
, Badu babu
Narsingh Ram welding
Sarfaraz Ahmed Sewing
Sibdayal ram carpenter section
Debendra nath mishra after His death satya Narayan Ray,both ex inmates as painting Instructor.

Leather and tanning Instructor, A local person from hudhudu near by place

Hiraman Ram .Fitter Instructor from Noora.

Civil work fakir mohammad from madai

Gosala work Bishunia gop and kisun Ram gop from madai village

Book binding, A local man from Hazaribagh town.

All training was offered in first hour and second hour and then was school education from 2 oclock in.school.The school comprised of teaching classes and big voluminous library was in operation for the education through the class room teaching.

Class hour started with prayer as follows

E jag data viswa vdhata, he sukh shanty niketan he............There were . school teachers as follows

Bijay kumar Srivastava . Head master
Raghab saran Sharma, teacher
A hanan, teacher
A nasim, teacher
And language teachers in Bengali, oriya and hindi from house masters.The school used to be

closed at 5 .

House masters were teachers in evening and night hours duty with inmates whose name was as below
.Jasoda nandan das from purulia

Lingraj rath from odisha,

Kasinath mishra from odisha.

Danodar nishra from odisha transferred to odisha

Sashi bhusan Rath from odisha

Sital Prasad singh from chapra

Shyam bihari singh from arrah.

Kunja lal banerjee from cuttack

A hansada from birbhum

Chandra sekhar singh from Bihar

Md yusuf ali from hazaribagh

Muralidhar Sharma from madai

Raghunandan Prasad from gaya,

A hamid sidikki from chapra

gopi nath verma from Hazaribagh who was district coordinator of scouts and guide.

Ram lakhan jha from darbhanga

Jagdish Prasad jha from Bhagalpur

Amin ali from hazaribagh lakhe

Sattar ali from lakhe. Both were brothers

Phanindra mukherjee from burdwan

Laxman Prasad from Hazaribagh

Abdul Latif (housemaster) from Sasaram

Ravindra Kumar Topo from Lohardaga, Ranchi

Siddhanath Prasad (housemaster)

Ram Sagar Pathak (housemaster)
Shivsagar Pathak
Shyam Narayan Pathak

Hospital staffs
D n mallik Doctor 1930 from hazaribagh
B nandi Doctor
Sudarsan singh Doctor 1957-63
B chaterjee Doctor 1963-65
Rn bhattacharya 1965 68
Narayan tripathi compounder from odisha
1930-40
Sib Prasad mahapatra from odisha 1940
1958
Rewa Ram dresser from hazaribagh
Ram dhan dresser from hazaribagh
Matrons lady.
Sudha sinha 1951 56
Bhagya wati devi 1956 1968

Peons
Bandhan Ram from noora
Bodhan Ram from hazaribagh
Neman Ram from madai
Parikhit Ram from madai
Sakur ahmed from madai
dinu ram
Bhukhan ram from hazaribagh
Ramji from deoghar
Nandu lal store assistant

Clerical staffs

Ambika Prasad Head clerck
Rameswar Prasad clerck from hazaribagh
Paras nath thakur from deoghar
Jugal kishore Prasad from hazaribagh
A sanga from hazaribagh
Parmeswar Ram from hazaribagh
Sivji tiwari from samastipur
Charu Chandra mukherjee steno to
superintendant
After him kaushal kishore srivastav steno.
Girbar Prasad, The cadre included store
work also in which he was working

Chief wardens, as major responsible
officers,

S Demta 1946 - 1949
Madhusudan mishra from odisha 1949 to
1960
Gopinath verma 1960 63

Deputy superindentants
Sanat kumar basu 1925 31
Jawahar Prasad
jogindra nath mishra 1955- 1960
c p n sinha 1961- 64
A srivastav 1965 68s

Superintendants
M wester 1924 31
MG Mitra
CPN Sinha

Hrudaya narayan thakur 1954-1959
Ram babu mishra 1959- 1960
Jogindra nath mishra 1961-1964
Ram babu mishra 1964- 65
Bandhu Prasad 1966- 1970
Ram babu mishra 1970 till Reformatory
school collapsed

Probationer officers
Rajdeo Prasad
Nabal kishore Sharma
In addition a project in the name of pilot
centre was opened by the Bihar government
in a
constructed building near lake 3 and 4.
Senior psychologist , and 4 junior
psychologist were
posted .2 psychologist Rameswar Prasad
singh and vidya bhusan seth were given
quarters at
reformatory school staff colony. These
staffs were associated with psychologist test
of inmates of
reformatory school. This project was
operative in 1956-57.Senior psychologist
was class1 officer
equivalent to the superintendant of reformat
ory school. He always was eager to be posted as
reformatory school having big infra
structure.The reformatory school became target
of conflict

51

on governance. Due to separation of states after independence ,number of convicts and amount of budget reduced.Bihar government could not understand importance of the reformatory act and school at hazaribagh. It was converted as esidential girls school in restricted area of campus but staffs were transferred to other places.The post office was shifted from the campus.Farm land, work shop, staff colony quarter collapsed due to no management.The play ground which was best fo matches in district being used by inmates is lost one. Cattle infra structure collapsed.Today dormitories, school. Gymnasium, hospital campus store, kitchen yards etc are of no use due to lock up to protecy girl student.The pilot centre office near lake is press club of india.The walls and security tombs are collapsing Tomb for Security Staff

The walls of the reformatory jail now under collapse for non purpose utilization walls with warden quarter is given for readers purpose.

The workshop with costly machines are abandoned with lockup which were established for training of the delinquents. Such big infrastructure was damaged without use and utility.This four state agreement in british government failed after independence.my self messaged to MP j sinha to invite attention of central government to use campus with infrastructure for union territories convicted delinquents instead of making it residential school of the girls.Now the government never thought of the building, training and education of the juvenile delinquents. On the contrary legislations after independence did not think of infrastructure and education for reformations.This was gora jail and CRP centre and the governments never protected lost institution which was glory of hazaribagh for its beauty and heritage.

Similarily there was a big sweeper colony consistin of the sweeping staffs of around 30 families. These sweeping staffs had residential quarters with tap water facility as provided to other stffs. The inside reformatory jail ,the water facility was given from lake waters being refined through coke system long back.Subsequently wwater supply was given from chadwa dam. A water tank

was stationed near staff colony of the reformatory school.When many in town had not water

facility, reformatory school campus had tap water facility given by the staffs of the government water supply department.Last water supply man opening key in tank was chohan ram from madai.

We need to appreciate also Reformatory
school act brought by the Britishers for youthful
offenders who were subjected to reformation
by the provisions of the act by way of special
training given to them for future
employment. As a matter of fact provision of
Act 6 was very
categorical for sufficient number of inmates
were necessary in night hours. Therefore four
numbers of big Dormitories were constructed
as huge buildings connected with central house
known as gol ghar. Four dormitories at
distances were joined in round concrete roof
roads for
passage to dormitories who were being
locked up before 7 oclock in evening having
taken food
and offering prayer program me in front of
gol ghar.

Dormitory no.3 attached to gol ghar now
renovated where Indira Gandhi residential
school girls are staying. Author visited the place
after 50 years.and talked to girl students.

Chinmay sarkar , Head master, ANNADA
SCHOOL IS PRESENT.

Entry road to reformatory school from lake near playground.

The prayer sound was being heard at a

distance of 4 to 5 kilometers out side the campus .Nig ht teachers were allotted to accompany the

inmates in night duty by the warden of the reformatory school who was duty bound to be present

with staffs in golghar before locking of the dormitories after pocket check of the individual

inmates by teachers allotted in night dormitories. This arrangement as routine practice was in

compliance of the act 6 where sufficient inmates together in night was mandatory. As night

teachers were accompanying the inmates, they were designated as house masters. They were also

locked with the residential delinquents in night hours for which inmates had a deep feeling of

affection and respect as their guardians. Entire process of locking up to late evening or night was

being supervised by the warden till the system is complete. Dormitories were very big having

cots and bed with toilets, water, light. large numbers of sweepers were provided residence near

58

colony for cleaning of toilets regularly.Similarily the unlocking or opening was in early dark

morning under the supervision of the warden . The inmates after exit from dormitories with bath

and joint breakfast system were given allotments for working in farms, workshops,etc based on

monthly calendar wise allotment drawn by the warden. There were several occasion when in

night hours have fled jumping from dormitories and walls cutting iron rods brought from

workshops in hidden manner and warden was charged accountable in the institution.

GOL GHAR WAS EARLIER connected WITH dormitories AT first floors the second provision in manual was regular daily visit of the superintendent, deputy

superintendent and warden at 10 AM with selective staffs to entire in side performing places to

observe the performances of the inmates. For farming workers a weekly program me of visit of

this officers were being made to ascertain the deficiency of irrigation, variety performance,

protection arrangements of the farms. Two farms were near lake 4 and 2 respectively of 100 acres each with full water facility. Each farm had employed gardeners with 24 hours presence. They

were given house to stay. Gardens with mali were watching stock out side the campus. The farms

had bushy boundary. The source of irrigation of first farm was adjacent lake two connected to a

pump house protected in a constructed house. T he water was drawn from lake for irrigation of the

crops .Th production was huge for cow dung organic fertilizer from dairy farm .The produce were

used for vegetable purpose of the inmates .The farm adjacent to lake 4 was termed tandeli . This

was main farm of the rice production in khariff and millets during Rabi season .The kolghati farm

was having two boring wells for irrigation purpose through pulley system. The main production here

was vegetables, red gram ,millets. The boundary wall from central jail to kolghati was brick wall

and from water tank to kolghati village was bushy enclosures by the side of the road connecting staff colony of the Reformatory school and kolghati. Additionally , there was a big garden of the deputy

superintendent attached to post office called Reformatory school post office. This farm was having mali madho mahto from sindur village. Of Hazaribagh . After his retirement one Gardner was appointed

to manage the farm which had fruit and flower garden with a portion with vegetables. The farm

attached to lake 2 was managed by sukar mali from silwar vllage. The kolghatti farm was looked

by bhattu mali son of sukar mali.The farm at the side of lake 4 was managed by cheddi ram from Kolghatti village and

after his retirement his son by zakir mohamad .As a whole . constructed for home less persons by the government near by the central jail boundary. agricultural training by the

inmates was big experience in agriculture training sectors by the inmates for their future.s

A FARM NEAR KOLGHATTI, NOW WITH HOUSES WITH P M GRIH NIVAS

YOJNAS was constructed for housing of the home less person by the government .Now the lands in major portion are abandoned and fallow lands which was controlled by the Reformatory school...

The gardeners were
sukar mahto from slwar
bhatu mahto

61

madho mahto from sindur
chedi ram mohamad from kolghati
zakir hussain from kolghati
now lands are transferred to other institution
with close institution with broken residences
warden quarter of late madhu sudan mishra
and broken quarters are given in the book.

Kolghati Farm abandoned

Group discussion with the girls of the residential

school in 2022

2. International Institutions of the Reformatory School

The Reform school was a penal institution mainly for the teen agers in the United Kingdom and its colonies, in between the year1830- 1900. In 1852 concept of Reformatory school in similar concept with slight modification came to recognitions. This concept was meant for youngsters who were convicted of crimes as an alternative to adult prisoners. In similar way industrial schools were opened for the purpose of protection of the children. Both systems were measures in between 1857- 1930.They were recognized schools. Both United Kingdom and united states of America adopted these provisions. Both United Kingdom and united states of America became worried of social matters in the cities after industrialisation on poverty, immigration and vagrancy. There was a shift of policy from retribution to reform. In the late 19th and early 20th century, United states of America found faulty practice in dealing with the juvenile offenders. They saw same methodology as dealt with adult criminals with that of juveniles. It was found that juveniles were sexually exploited by older inmates and were following directions of the hard criminals as inmates. As a consequence, sentenced offenders as deterrent for future crimes, the released offenders instead of being reformed, they were involved in more criminal acts in future. This resulted in change of policy. An approach for separate juvenile court, for the offenders for them who did not reach major age, and building of separate institution for juvenile's delinquents was thought with rehabilitation policy of released inmates. These institutions were custodial and were Reform schools. In United Kingdom Reformatory schools were built up for criminal children with infra structure of industrial schools. This was done to protect vulnerable criminal children from future activities of the crimes. There was a rise in juvenile delinquency in early 19th century. So, Parliament set up a committee for looking to cause of increasing juvenile delinquency in 1837 for juvenile crimes in the streets of the metropolis writer Charles Dickens published an article Oliver Twist relating to the child concerned with street gang. This was in 1846 and soon after juvenile offence act 1846 was introduced in which children under 14 were made to be tried in special court but not in adult court. Magistrate had to send children to industrial schools to learn skills so that they can be employable. This was to associate giving education also and to keep children away from old aged prisoners. The power to create such establishment was made 1 in 1854.This was termed Reformatory schools built up by 1857.This was also joined as industrial schools by an act.

In Australia Reform schools were established by the neglected and criminal children Act 1864.As per the act the children under guardian ship of the state were sent to Industrial school as neglected child but who broke law were sent to the Reformatory school. Subsequently due to overcrowding and poor sanitation during stay period it became public issue. Inmates had to suffer from measles and eye diseases which was

65

thought for above strength inmates. Therefore, reform school concept in 1887 came to an end in that country. But unlike Australia, infra structures of reformatory schools in United Kingdom were better and continued for long period including opening of such institution in India and Hazaribagh remained as model institution with representations from four states, Bihar, Bengal. Assam and Odisha, then states in India. In U. K. one of the schools is given here at Adel in England. The school was Leeds Reformatory school for Boys opened in 1857 in the rural areas of the Adales. The school was run by the Leeds society for the reformation of the juvenile offenders. The location of the school was rural area and this was because the Victorians felt that cities were dangerous places, full of bad influences, and being out in te country side would children to be well behaved and hard working. This selection of location was principle and value based as evident from opening of Reformatory school away from then small city of Hazaribagh near central jail having workshops of various trades. The Leeds Reformatory school Adales had a shoe maker's shop, a joiner's shop, a smith's shop, and a gas house as well as a number of farm yard animals. The school had 3 acres of land fixed for training on growing crops, the school had its own bands well as football and gymnastics teams. The school had its own swimming pool created in 1888. The Victorians used to think that by taking parts in sports, the young children may get moral values being away from crimes. The boys leaving the school were apprenticed in fishing boats at Grimsby. By that school was also proud of the boys.

Recent publications from Yerwada, Pune reported by Chinmay Damale dated 2nd November, 2023, on juveniles of Reformatory learn the joy of gardening, is evidence of another Reformatory school which was established near central prisons at Yerwada in Maharashtra is stated that this school was established in 1889 with 60 boys. The boys mostly were employed in gardening. It says effect of incarceration of the children in 19th century reformatories have been topic of some interest. some scholars have opined that the reformation stresses on social control that injures and harms children more than the help they get as child running away from law and who nearly in digest than criminal. it is reported that in the flower show of 1911 organized by Agric- Horticultural society, Pune, Reformatory school, Yerwada exhibited many varieties of capsicum, tomatoes, custard apple, and pumpkin, and won first prize for the former two and third prize for latter two. The young gardeners' children aged between14- 18 was felicitated by the official of the Agric-horticulture society.it was announced that society would give donation to the Reformatory school as a gesture of appreciation. Reformatory school Yerwada was established in June 1889 with 60 boys juvenile offenders belonging to the criminal tribes. Amaravati, Secunderabad, Karachi, and Kaira offenders were being housed there. By 1910, The inmate strength increased to 300 yearly. The goal of Reformatory was to make juvenile offenders to earn a good life by some sorts of earning by gardening or apprentice

67

training earned by them. It was thought to keep inmates engaged and busy. The mandate was for juvenile offenders to allow them to earn an honest livelihood by some sort of calling gardening, carpentry, black smith, painting, tailoring, book binding etc. Training given to them. In 1902 it was planned to give formal education here. Class rooms were made. They were taught science, mathematics. English etc.12 acres of land was provided near central prison, Yerwada just as Hazaribagh Reformatory school located near central jail, Agriculture farm made were training place for inmates for production of cereals and vegetables. An instructor for agriculture was deputed by state 2 days weekly Class room teaching and farming was main choices of learning. The awards of horticulture society as stated above speaks of performance as compared to other common citizens of Pune on performance ability of the delinquents about their reformed conducts and efficient earning ability. The training how to earn and how to reform was exemplary contribution of the Britishers in adopting this act in their country as well as in India. Present acts of reforms are NGO and club based non-government organization are not worth of quality and efficiency as given in Reformatory school of Hazaribagh and other places. The playground of Reformatory school, Hazaribagh and gymnasium were classic in nature. The foot ball matches with St. Xavier's school. YMCA, Police club. Other clubs were witnessed by the town people. Most of the time THE winners were Reformatory school boys who were talented. The gymnasium with drills were of high standard. Instructors were being engaged from among house Amal Krishna Basu eminent advocate used to give directions in annual drama with engaged dancers from town for giving training. It was so impressive that dance shown in stage by one I inmate amidst flowers in stage was beautiful presentation of Indian art which superintendent Mr. Wester could not digest who was a British officer and had restricted dance in drama for coming years. Therefore, a beneficial and useful act in India was introduced for the benefit of juvenile delinquents under Reformatory school act in British India. Hazaribagh was chosen a place for the same near central jail. This was destination of major four states of eastern India. This collapsed though the infra structure could be a heritage without maintenance the heritage institution is at a stage of collapse. Policy holders had no idea of these beautiful institution built up in international concept. Before we take up degradation, we should look to primitive approach in international level. We need to know some of the primitive institutes for a better policy and that the institutes are soon revived soon in India. A historical back ground about growth of reformatory school have been collected and presented below for the categorical analysis of the readers and their interest in upkeeping of this heritage institution in the interest of reduction child criminality as well as restoration of skill development policy for offenders so that they have earning ability being released from the schools' Balram Kumar Gupta. Director, Academics while speaking on 28th April ,2018 at Chandigarh on J J Act 2015 had said, it is easier to build strong children. it is difficult to repair a broken child.

There was direction of the supreme court in the matter of Sampoorna Behera vs. Union of India in 2018 to translate and implement legal framework. Both central and state governments should ensure all positions in NCPCR and SCPCR a filled-up valentine. It was directed for provision for adequate staffs to statutory bodies, Different bodies related should take duty effectively, study should be made on existence of probation officers, Police to properly understand the role as done by the child. Honorable justice spoke on probation and rehabilitations of the child. Therefore, the question was before framer of policy on various acts of free India connected with juvenile justice system when Reformatory school act was available in India. This had all infra structures of skill developments brought from England as seen in Hazaribagh Reformatory school. There was a need to go to backgrounds of international institutions where many had Reformatory schools. Many collections here have been brought in the matter being collected. Many world countries have their history on juvenile delinquency justice as suited to their own situations. In united states of America, it originates from eighteenth century preferably from 1889.In German it starts from 1870.It started in France little late from 1912.Earlier the child offenders were being punished as adult. Most of the countries changed their policy of child justice as adult one. While doing so age was decided as a factor to differentiate between adult and child by many countries. The age to
70

define child changed. India was ruled by Britain in 19th century. Therefore, British rule was to be adopted here. So, the history of English law in the juvenile delinquency needs to be known for readers. Accordingly, the rule collection was felt necessary.

The collected materials are not more. Many old Reformatory schools giving service then are not in pictures. Very less reference is available for the purpose. The crimes of juveniles are in increasing trend. So, our efforts to project selective and un noticed institutions. We shall present here for records and references before we evaluate the role of the government as well as related organizations Following information are placed in this chapter for awareness and knowledge of the readers.

COLLECTED MATERIALS OF JUVENILE DELIQUENCY IN ENGLAND ETC.

Philanthropic Society's 'Female Reform' and new chapel c.1805 © Peter Higginbotham

In the first part of the nineteenth century, penalties for those found guilty of crimes would, by modern standards, be considered exceptionally severe. In 1833, a boy of 9 was sentenced to death (though not actually executed) for stealing 2d worth of paint. Two boys of 15 were transported for seven years for stealing a pair of boots. Such treatment began to be questioned and in 1837 Parkhurst prison was used to provide an experimental reformatory regime for young offenders. They were provided with outdoor industrial training, combined with school instruction and religious teaching. The establishment had mixed results and closed in 1864, with the authorities indicating that private or charitably run establishments were preferable for such purposes.

In 1846, Lord Houghton attempted to introduce a parliamentary bill to establish a reformatory schools system. Although the bill did not become law, it led to growing interest in such a scheme. The Philanthropic Society was again at the forefront of the movement. In 1849, after visiting the agricultural colony for delinquent boys at Mettray in France, the Society established a pioneer farm colony for boys at Redhill in Surrey.

Rickyard at Philanthropic Society's Farm School, Redhill, c.1920 © Peter Higginbotham

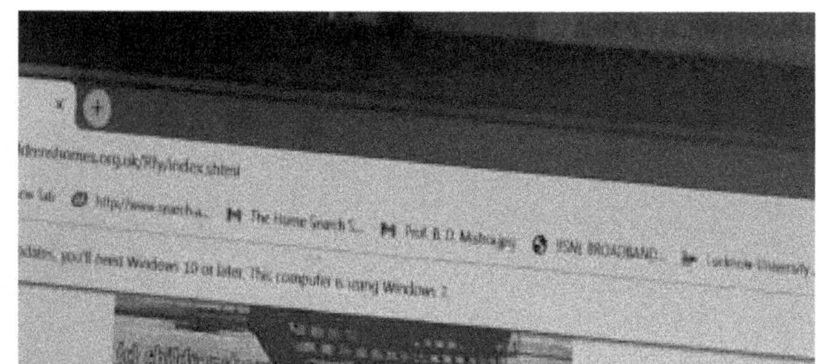

The Cornwall, c 1910. © Peter Higginbotham

In 1899, the initial prison requirement for those entering a Reformatory was abolished. The difference between Reformatory Schools and Certified Industrial Schools was then diminish although the latter broadly dealt with children who were younger and included those who we deemed to be in danger of becoming criminals rather than necessarily having committed off

Some reformatories had an associated Auxiliary Homes. These were usually small homes wh either catered for particularly difficult cases, or were used as a half-way house for inmates wh were about to leave to go into employment.

The majority of the both Reformatory and Industrial Schools were privately run, often by religio groups. For a variety of reasons, some proved unable to operate successfully and closed with few years. For example, a Reformatory was opened in 1856 by the monks of St Bernard's Abb at Whitwick in Leicestershire. The school, or 'agricultural colony' was took up to 250 delinquent Roman Catholic boys and was run with the help of lay assistants. However, the staff were unat to control their charges. There were several riots and in 1878 after sixty boys escaped, after attacking the master in charge with knives stolen from the dining room. The establishment was closed in 1881 after its certificate was withdrawn.

3. Present Juvenile Act, 2015—Not a Solution

The 2015 passed an act considering the heinous crime at Dehi called Nirbhaya case, is no doubt a law felt improved but its specific applications as compared to Reformatory act is neither transparent nor practical in application. The law is applicable as per clause article 15 (3), with two categories
Children in conflict of law
Children with care and protection
The need of amendment on age, their trial, and treatment was felt necessary and was made 2015 act made formation of JJB in each district and to dispose cases of juveniles as per the requirements. The act provides after care programs and provision of observation home, special home, children homes for care of juveniles. T his act also speak of rehabilitation, reintegration in the society. It also say of care and protection. It also uses various machinery during hearing of case and provides shelter homes even during hearing. Article 39 (e), (f), 45 and 47 of the constitution. The child is defined who has not attended age of 18 under section 2 (12). Child in conflict of law is protected under section 2 9 13) AND CHILD protected under section 2 (14) are on care and protection. As per out line juvenile justice board will dispose the case The duties and

responsibility are mentioned in the section 8. Grant of bail is under section 12. Child welfare committee is covered in section 27 and rehabilitation and re integration is covered in section 39. The act covers children health, safety, development and vulnerability.
Now the question is on remedy period to be decided, who are the authorities to deal and decide within period of child definition. Certain matters are decided till decision from supreme court and by the period of final decision, the child is adult or whether he can be reformed in such long time when parents, guardian prolong the disputes for long time and many also escape punishment. There are many decisions in the matter from various courts for example highest court has said that board during did not consult psychologist before decision, the matters if the trial should be as child or adult and in many cases age disputes prolong cases. Thus, objective of reformation and rehabilitation of offenders is not possible. The ambiguity never persisted in reformatory school act where reformation and rehabilitation were practical, object oriented and no unnecessary litigation issue delaying child to come to main stream though he some time acted badly due to the circumstance.
In this matter, a case by human rights commission Odisha is presented here. This part of the document shown as order from National Human right commission which did not come as option as settled policy in the matter. The judgement obtained bu the RTI activist has been noted below for the consumption of the Readers

.The issue was related to the minor gang rape during the year 2020 and victim murdered.

This was a shameful event so far our cultural integrity and values of national and international repute was shaken and this also confirms that juveniles are no way lesser than adults in committing offenses of such serious nature. The degeneration of our social values in the life of Indian community was badly defamed at the international level. Therefore laxity that their juveniles cannot be construed without exemplary punitive action under the law of this nation.

Some modifications though were made in the 2015 juvenile act. But such corrections without appropriate juvenile homes and without accountability of the governments who has to take responsibility for the reformation and rehabilitation of the juveniles, the aspiration and objective of dealing juvenile delinquents will remain unfulfilled.

In this background some of the judicial process and court order are being placed here which will confirm that the juveniles case should also be treated seriously and the courts like human right commission and other similar courts have no answer to this type of problem. Accordingly some facts and judgements are extracted below for the readers to have their own view in the matter but ultimately the nation has to think of juvenile homes and values of corrections for the juveniles appropriately.

Diary No	18218/IN/2020	Case / File No	1285/34/17/2020
Victim Name	MINOR GANG RAPE VICTIM MURDERED	Registration Date	02/12/2020

Action List (Click on Action given in blue color to view details)

Action No.	Action	Authority	Action Date
6	**Concluded and No Further Action Required**		12/07/2022
5	**Relief by Goverment**		12/07/2022
4	**Additional Information Called for**	THE DEPUTY COMMISSIONER	04/04/2022
3	**Additional Information Called for**	THE DEPUTY COMMISSIONER	10/01/2022
2	**Additional Information Called for**	THE SUPERINTENDENT OF POLICE	31/03/2021
1	**Action Taken Report Called for**	THE SUPERINTENDENT OF POLICE SP office Sahibganj, Jharkhand	07/12/2020

Expand All Action List

ction

Action : Concluded and No Further Action Required(Action No 6)

Action Date	12/07/2022
Authority	, Complainant Email * :
Procceeding	The Complainant alleged Kidnapping, gang rape and murder of minor girl. A case has been registered but the accused has not yet been arrested and there is no progress in the case. Vide proceedings 07.12.2020 the Commission took cognizance in the matter and directed to the Superintendent of Police, Sahibganj, Jharkhand to submit an Action Taken Report in the matter within 4 weeks. The Superintendent of Police, Sahibganj vide email dated 17.02.2021 forwarded an action taken report dated 07.01.2021 along with enquiry report of SDPO, Barharba. It was submitted in the report that a case vide Crime No. 118/20 dated 12.10.2020 u/s 302/376D/120B/201 IPC r/w 4/6 POSCO Act, was registered against five accused persons and all of them were arrested and sent to jail. A team of doctors was constituted which opined cause of death as Death was due to asphyxia as a result of strangulation by ligature. However, viscera have been preserved and above-mentioned sample have been called for further information. Violent sexual assault was committed on the person of the deceased before death. It was submitted that during investigation all allegations found true against accused persons and soon chargesheet will be filled. In response SP Sahib Ganj has submitted its report dated 25.02.2022 along with the report of Sub Divisional Police Officer dated 07/02/2022. The report reveals that charge sheet no.01/2021 dated 11.01.2021 u/s 302/376D/201/120B IPC r/w 4/6 POSCO Act has been filed in the court. All the accused are under judicial custody. Representation vide reference no. PS Ranga -470/21 dtd 27.05.2021 for compensation to the NOK of the victim has been forwarded, which is still pending. In pursuance to directions issued by the Commission on 04.04.2022, a report dated 18.04.2022 by the Dy. Commissioner, Saheb Ganj, Jharkhand has been received. The report specifies that the NOK/ father Sh. ████████, r/o ████████, PS

Complaint

Diary No	18218/IN/2020	Section	M-5
Language	ENGLISH	Mode	HRCNET/ONLINE
Received Date	14/10/2020	Complaint Date	14/10/2020

Victim

Victim Name	MINOR GANG RAPE VICTIM MURDERED		Gender	Unknown
Religion	Unknown		Cast	Unknown
Address	RANGA POLICE STATION AREA			
District	SAHIBGANJ		State	JHARKHAND

Complainant

Name	JAYANTA KUMAR DAS		
Address	SATYA NAGAR SIDHA MAHABIR PATANA		
District	PURI	State	ODISHA (752002)

Incident

Incident Place	RANGA P.S.AREA	Incident Date	11/10/2020
Incident Category	CHILD RAPE		
Incident District	SAHIBGANJ	Incident State	JHARKHAND
Incident Details			

It may be seen in the above case that a minor is raped and murdered and relief from Human right commission is prayed. Enquiry on information is received from police of the Jharkhand case. It is also noticed that victim parents have received ten lakhs from Jharkhand government but there was no judgement on the ground that matter is

under domain of the court The matter prolonged
for long time for collection of information and
remain undecided. If court was taking of the
matter why the human right commission
entertained application to take up the matter by
them and long time passed in the matter.
Otherwise, the court take long time though JJ
board was constituted in 2015 act specifically
for minor juveniles. The matter by human right
commission and court is duplications only.

Sanjeet vs. Haryana on 5th January Learned
counsel for the petitioner at the outset, submitted
that petitioner at this stage is being tried as adult.
Learned counsel for the [petitioner on …
application by trial court dismissed as
withdrawn with liberty to approach with liberty
for regular bail if petitioner surrenders before 15
01 2023 This shows case in the matter is in two
courts. Obviously time-consuming matter in the
matter of child case. This is conflicting and
time-consuming loosing reformation policy.
This order was in Punjab and Haryana high
court. This decision was on 5 01 2023though
juvenile board had rejected bail earlier as
juvenile case.
In Sahil Chadar vs. Madhya Pradesh on April
28, 2021 Madhya Pradesh high court said
applicant is aged about 17. It is not known as to
whether the applicant is being tried as adult or
as a juvenile Under the fact and circumstances
of the case, this court is of …5 10 2020 passed
by the principal judge, juvenile justice board,
Bhopal in crime no 402 /2020 registered at
police station Misrod district, Bhopal for offence
under 302 and 201 of I. P. C. as well as order
81

…(care and protection of children) act 2015 as well as appeal has been rejected, This is again conflict and not timely.

While taking up the issue in this chapter, he was happy to witness the order of the supreme court in the case of Shilpa Mittal vs. state (NCT of Delhi) and another on Jan 9, 2020. In short… should be tried as adult. The appeal filed to the children court was also dismissed on 11 2 2019.There after the juvenile X through his mother approached the high court of Delhi, which vide…. adult, even if the children court holds that that child has to be tried as adult, it must ensure that final order includes an individual care plan, for rehabilitation of the child as specified…a children has to be tried as an adult. It has also been provided that though the child may be tried as an adult, reformative process services, educational services, skill development, alternate therapy council…necessary as the judge concluded.

37. In passing we may note that in the impugned judgement the name of the child in conflict of law, has been disclosed. This is not in accordance with the provisions of Section 74 of the 2015 act, and various judgements of the courts. We direct the High Court to correct the judgement and remove the name of the child in conflict with law.

38. We further direct that a copy of this judgement be sent to the Secretary of Law, Ministry of Law and Justice, Government of India, Secretary, Home, Ministry of Women and Child Development, Government of India and the Secretary, Home, Ministry of Home Affairs, and Registrar General, Delhi High Court, who

shall ensure that issue raised in this judgement is addressed by the Parliament as early as possible or by the Executive by issuing an Ordinance. Our directions shall continue to remain in force only till such action is taken.

39. Pending application(s), if any, stand(s) disposed of.

The juvenile justice (CRN protection of children) act 2015, JJ act as several lacunae including on the nature of crimes, more particularly heinous crimes. The heinous crimes in this act have not been well defined and even the quantum of punishment has not been adequately covered to be imposed on the offender considering the nature of crime. This creates conflict for example whether a 16-year-old should be imprisoned for 7 years in theft cases is a matter of decision, cannot be solved with transparency.

Similarly, the legislation of act 2015 can be used as per convenience taking the situations for example if a lady files a rape case against a boy and when a boy and girl have physical relationship the girl's father files a rape case against the boy. In such a situation the children will be punished and this will not be fair in the eye of the law.

There are also other issues. The juvenile records once created under conflict of law will be a record which may influence the career of the minor. Magistrates dealing with the case do not have training in the matter of child rules for their protection. There is requirement that child welfare committee, JJB district protection unit and police must have a proper coordination in between them. The juvenile justice act

83

amendment never reports any abuse or cruelty by the staffs of the child care institutions. The imprisonment between 3 and 7 years are non-cognizable cases. There are many adoption cases pending before the court and proceedings of the court rapid and fast. The power is transferred to magistrates. Earlier the act 2000 provided trials of juveniles with low age but this act has created ambiguity by the courts to decide nature of heinous crimes for sixteen- to eighteen-year-old children to be dealt as adult offender.

There are many other ambiguities relating to classification of age. The act divides age in two categories. One before 16 and other between 16-18. Though efforts are made to improve the law but obstacles are many. The decision during the process of legal recourse has to be made if the trial has to be made as child or an adult considering nature of allegation and then trial proceeds. Many responsibilities have been entrusted to juvenile justice board. The board will go in to nature of case then decide age,

As per 2011 census data, children between the ages 7 to 18years constitutes about 25 % of the total population. According to NCRB, National crime record bureau. The percentage of juvenile crime as a proportion of total crime has increased 1 % to1.5%. FRM 2003 TO 2022. 16 TO 18 YEARS OLD ACCUSED OF CRIME AS A PERCENTAGE OF ALL JUVENILE/ CHILD ACCUSED OF CRIME FROM 54 % TO 70 % FROM 2003 TO 2022.

Few important features of the act.

Compulsory registration of the institution

Presumption and determination of age

4. Crime Status of Juvenile Delinquents in India and its Growth

The data available states that there is 7.6 % increase in crime don ne by the juvenile offenders who are defined as minors in 2021.There were 2455 juvenile crimes noticed in the year. It rose to 2643 in the year 2921, The murder crimes done in various foreign is not less and differs in the number. The countries are united states 8226, Russia 7885, Columbia 12834, Brazil 20388.In the capital city of India, New Delhi there were 1859 cases of crimes during the year 2021.After new Delhi, next position was Surat with over 1.6 thousand criminal cases in that year.

In Assam in the year 2021 the crime rate in per one lakh population was 86.4% which was maximum followed by Tripura, 62 %. Followed with that it was 46.1% in west Bengal and Haryana 49.4%s and Arunachal Pradesh 41.7. If we analyze the status of crime in 2016, New Delhi happens to be the state which is not safe maximum. The data reports highest cognizable crime rate in India. 160.4 per one lakh people. The minimum juvenile crime rate is from Nagaland. Representing percentage share. In international era out of 170 countries India is positioned at 148 under peace, women, security index. Similarly in 2021 total 31170 cases were registered during 2021. This was increase of 4.7 % as against crimes of the year 2020.The number of cases registered were 29768 in 2020. Out of this number 76.2 % were 28539 in the age between – 18 years with increasing rate of crime from 6.7% to 7 % by the end of the year 2022.The increase in crime rate is known to policy makers who did not understand transformations like Reformatory act to transformation under apprentice training. Indian parliament is witness to the status which during adoption of act 2015 on juvenile justice care and protection of children in 2015 faced serious concerns of the members in the house. There were protests from among the members on provisions of child right. Members were not satisfied with the bill and had demanded more amendments.

The retention of children as juvenile crimes was a critical issue in the central territory at present also. There are not central jails for crimes in Andaman microbar, Dadra and Nagar haveli, Daman and Diu, Lakshadweep. Therefore, the concept of juvenile crime retention house is remote. Recently necessity of more juvenile justice board has been felt under judicial scrutiny. But nobody is concerned on reformations with valid training institutions as was reformatory schools.

In 1996 there was a significant growth in juvenile delinquency as compared to other years. The arrests were 8478 per one lakh persons in between age from 10 to 17 years 'There was7.6 percent growth in that year. Similarly, there were 2455 juvenile crimes during the year which increased and were 2843 during the year 2021.In

86

between these years a trend of growth of crimes connected with murder and attempt to murder was seen.78 cases of murder
And 154 cases of attempt to murder was noticed.

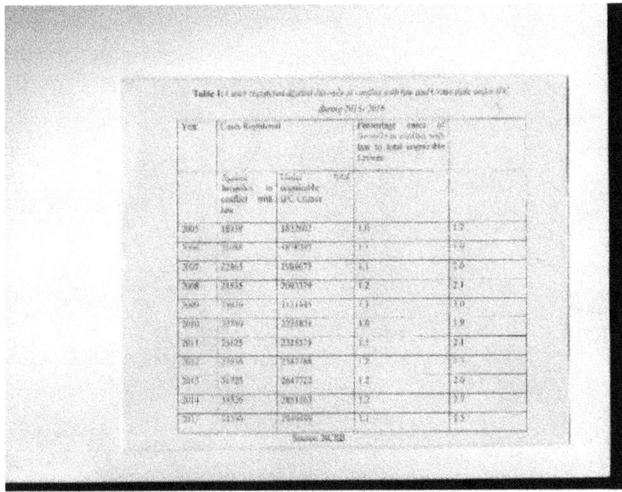

Table 1: [illegible] registered against juveniles in conflict with law and accountable under IPC during 2015-2016

Year	Cases Registered		Percentage cases of Juveniles in conflict with law to total accountable Crimes	
	Juveniles in conflict with law	Under accountable IPC Crimes	Total	
2005	[illegible]	[illegible]	1.1	1.2
2006	[illegible]	[illegible]	1.1	1.0
2007	22465	[illegible]	1.1	2.6
2008	24535	[illegible]	1.2	2.1
2009	[illegible]	[illegible]	1.1	2.0
2010	[illegible]	[illegible]	1.0	1.9
2011	25125	[illegible]	1.1	2.1
2012	[illegible]	[illegible]	1.2	2.1
2013	[illegible]	[illegible]	1.2	2.6
2014	[illegible]	[illegible]	1.2	2.7
2015	[illegible]	[illegible]	1.1	2.5

Source: NCRB

About forty thousand of juveniles were arrested for various nature of the offences in 2019. Similarly, 31170 cases were registered in 2021 against juveniles. The age s between 16- 17 and also 18 were found to be major cases committing offences. This has been confirmed from the figures taken by national crime bureau, India.

The data of jail children in the age group of 16-18 during the year 2018-2020 showed 45 males and one female from Assam in 2019 with no data in 2020.The Bihar state had 55 mal and one female in the same year. Gujarat state had only 48 male jail inmates during this year. In Jharkhand it was one where as Karnataka it had

87

three male inmates in the same year. In Maharashtra it was 11 during this year but declined in 2019- 20.

Regarding crime committed by the juvenile state wise from Maharashtra during 2018, 2019, 2020 was 5880, 5189, 4079 respectively. Population in lakhs during 2011 was 361.1. Rate of crime juvenile was 11.3 percent in 2020. It was maximum in number as compared to other states having total cases between 19000 to 20000 in the whole country during the period. The data of other states I listed below.

Similarily disposal of cases arrested and sent to jails in 2009 in india varied from state to state. In Andhra Pradesh in 2009, there were 1565 cases of arrest and sent to courts under IPC and SLL CRIMES. 2218 persons were sent to homes as per advice of the administration. 212 were sent to the special jails.In Bihar during the year, 1066 were sent to jails, 154 were sent to the special jails. In Chhatisgarh it was more. 3112 cases were sent to jails and 619 persons went to special jails. In Gujarat 2466 cases were sent to courts in 2009 and 41 cases were referred to homes and others were handed over to the parents. In haryana 1374 were sent to courts and I case was referred to the home with 2 cases handed over to the parents.In maharastra it was 6972 cases referred to the courts but 979 cases sent to homes and 1768 were handed to the parents. In Rajasthan 2456 cases were referred to the court during the year with 246 cases referred to homes. The cases referred to courts in Tamil Nadu was 2921 where as 64444448 cases were sent to the homes. In the same year 32773 cases were sent to the courts. 4819 referred to homes and 4753 cases handed over to the parents in various states togather. In union territories 869 cases were sent to the courts and 167 cases to homes when 69 cases were handed over to the parents. In 2008 reports of juveniles under different SLL CRIMES show maximum 106 from madhya pradesh connected with arms act. With total 265 cases from various states. In the same state 359 cases were on gambling act with total of 779 cases from various states.In Delhi during 2023, reported murder cases were 92,286 connected with assault cases, theft 866, robbery 235 and 33 armed acts. In 2022 more than 1894 fresh cases against minors were pending in trial courts.The disposal of cases are very low. Since 2021, the cases left waiting for trial are 5128. 729 cases were sent to correction homes and others released. In2022 more than 1894 cases fresh o minors are pending in trial courts. There are rising cases in railway station thefts, and assault cases preferably from delhi.Therefore, rising crimes are issues of importance but government policy on correction home ignoring reformatory school act is no solution where future were amended with vocational trainings having infrastructures as was available in Hazaribagh Reformatory school now restricted in limited zone to a girl residential school.

Number of crimes of juveniles in top position are from 13 states of the country. In Madhya Pradesh it was 60000, Maharastra 55852, Delhi 24887, Rajasthan 24386, Tamil Nadu 24301,Gujarat 21368, Chhatisgarh 20062, Bihar 16452, Uttar Pradesh 12232, Haryana 11640, Andhra Pradesh 11353, Odisha 10802,

89

Telangana 10567. This was the data during 2013-2022. Stark rise in children crimes from 2014 to 2022 with reported cases was from 189423 to 162449 which marks 81% rise from 2014 to 2022.

There are reports on age group of juveniles apprehended in various cases from 1998 to 2008 as noted below. This also confirms ratio of boys and girls.

The tabular information of the juvenile apprehended under IPC from the year 1998 to 2008 have been placed in the next page
The table shows that in 1998 the activities of offences was also exhibited by the children between the age group of seven to twelve. The number in 1998 was 3336. Subsequently, yearwise presentation of the material data says that that is also an increasing trend. It was more in 1999 and the data was 4033. Somehow there is variation in reduction of the cases in some years but more or less the crime remains the activities of the children of the above group. The data in percentage of offences during 2007-2008 indicated low occurrence but it was seen that during the year 1996 and '97 the occurrence was very high i.e. 63%. All these confirms that offences of child is a continuous process and needs supervision, review and action so that the considerations of values and good conduct survives among children and they do not go bad with various types of offences.

TABLE-10.7

Juveniles Apprehended Under IPC And S.L. Crimes By Age Groups
(1998-2008)

Sl. No.	Year	7-12 Years	Percentage In Total	12-16 Years	Percentage To Total	16-18 Years	Percentage To Total	Total Apprehended
(1)	(2)	(3)	(4)	(5)	(6)	(7)	(8)	(9)
1	1998	3326	17.6	11544	61.0	4803	21.3	18923
2	1999	1019	21.5	10211	55.8	4110	22.3	8450
3	2000	2292	18.3	11380	56.3	1991	16.4	17982
4	2001*	3695	11.0	3759	57.9	17203	11.2	33698
5	2002	3688	12.5	13804	35.7	17427	48.7	25779
6	2003	3584	10.8	17867	55.1	8609	54.2	33330
7	2004	2107	6.9	20463	10.1	16021	53.1	26933
8	2005	1643	5.0	14090	43.3	17946	54.9	32681
9	2006	1395	5.0	13943	38.0	18315	56.8	32643
10	2007	1480	4.2	13114	25.3	20953	60.3	34527
11	2008	1381	3.7	13675	35.6	20954	60.7	34572
	PERCENTAGE CHANGE IN 2008 OVER 1998	-61.6		6.3		418.8		82.4
	PERCENTAGE CHANGE IN 2008 OVER 2007	-12.3		1.5		0.0		0.1

NOTE : 7-12 years means 7 years and above but below 12 years
* As Per New Definition Of Juvenile Justice Act, The Boys In The Age Group Of 16 - 18 Years Has Also Been Considered As Juveniles

Printed from

THE TIMES OF INDIA

Maharashtra ranks No. 1 in India in hard crimes by juveniles

TNN | Dec 23, 2019, 05.37 AM IST

MUMBAI: For the second year in a row, the biggest proportion of juveniles accused of hard crimes like murder and burglary is from Maharashtra, as per national crime records bureau (NCRB) data. Overall, the state is second, after Madhya Pradesh, when it comes to all crimes involving juveniles. Among cities, Mumbai is second, after Delhi, on this parameter.

Nevertheless, there has been a marginal decline in cases: Maharashtra recorded 116 cases of juveniles accused of murder in 2017—the last year for which NCRB has released data—compared to 130 in 2016.

There are701 juvenile justice board in country as the courts. With integrated child protection program assistance of the government of India the scheme is under operation but substantially did not yield fruitful results yet. The scheme belongs to women and child development. Despite facilities, the crime growth rate of juveniles was 4.7 % in 2021 as compared to 2020.Nain period was adolescents in which child involves in conflict of law. The supreme court of India while expressing concerns on crime growth rate of juveniles, observed that juvenile act 2015 has subserved its object. It observed we have gathered impression that leniency with which juveniles are dealt with in the name of goal of reformation is making them more and more emboldened in indulging in such heinous crimes. They expressed for failing to carve out an effective reform and rehabilitation policy for young offenders. Protection of children act 2015 known as juvenile justice act 2015 is not the option of reformation and rehabilitation as was available in British law which has started Reformatory school with massive infrastructure investments by creating large workshops, farms, schools and other training base. Reformatory school, Hazaribagh is one of the model to which neither state government nor central government realize its importance and mis used the infrastructures by making residential girls school in a jail structures built up then and could have been archeological structure of importances. The 2015 act which started with case of Nirbhaya incidence of Delhi held in 2012 it was found that out of 6 accused one escaped in the name of minor though committed offence as adult and the crime done was in adolescent stage. Therefore, he had no regards for law of the land and was not so child to be allowed for escape from the punishment. Democracy is not for crime and oppression where a child is 16 or

93

18. The parliament allowed voting age in 18 which was 21 earlier but allows escape from crime punishment considering them as juveniles. The information on juveniles apprehended in 2015 in IPC and SLL by age group offenders below age group   12 was 13 and cases done by age group between 12 – 16 was 283. The total cases committed by age group of 16 years was 796. All data were per lakhs of person totaling was 1092. Attempt to murder cases in the same year below 12 years age was10. Between 12- 16 years it was 342 where as it was 1008 between age boy of 16-18 years total cases in the year under same category was 1360.Culpable homicide cases in the year was 1 by below 12-year offenders. 15 cases were committed but age group of 12-16 years where as 41 cases done by all groups in the year having 25 done by age group of 16-18 years.

The figure is alarming. The crime made by 16-18 age group is higher. The tendency of doing crime originates from 12 years and below. Now a days thinker and activist the reason may be pornography and changing food habits. The sexual habits and uncontrolled biological impulses are the reason of juvenile crimes. I can cite that entire social disorders in society having no fear of punishment are the reasons as juvenile can better copy prisons doing unlawful; activities because of non-understanding of punishments as well as not knowing consequences. The poor upbringing in family may also be the reasons which parents do not understand how to build a child.

It is true that seminars and conferences elaborates in deliberation that child protection and counseling is necessary and acts is gift of circumstances but social evils for a child is also a family responsibility in educating children and punishment with reformation corrects future of the indiscipline children. Recent stone pelting, Naxalite activities, supply of weapons being encouraged by elders as seen in Kashmir and other places cannot be cause for child protection actions for such children who are badly guided by the elders of the society. The country cannot encourage child crime nor use liberal law without reformation.

Similarly increasing trend in juvenile crimes ranged between 2005- 15 increased. It varied from 18939 to 31 396 during the above period. This data was connected with offences under conflict of law. Under total cognizable offence the number varied from 1822602 to2949499. The percentage co relation of numbers between cases in conflict of law and total cognizable offence between the same period ranged from 1.0 to 1.1. The rate of crime between two categories ranged from1.7 to 2.5 in the same period.

figures of juveniles under IPC and SLL in 2015 included children between age 16 to 18. higher in number pornography and changing food behavior showed crimes on sex behavior more. Youngs are not able to control biological impulses due to hormonal changes. There are more rape cases in town areas as compared to the village areas.

There were 1.62 lakh cases of crimes against children in 2022.This was increase of 8.7 % as compared to 1.49 lakhs in 2021.There are reports that 3% of overall crimes are committed by the juveniles in india.so about one half of the Indian population are classified as juveniles in India. The decline in juvenile crime 285 was seen in 2020 as compared to 487.8 in 2021 and 385.5 in 2019. The crime rate above was in per lakh population.

Safest state on female crime is Tamil Nadu followed by Nagaland, which is lowest on incidence of crimes based on percentage share. India ranks 148 in world out of 170 countries in severity index on female crime rate. Uttar Pradesh and Delhi are having highest crime rates. Safest place is Coimbatore, Chennai. Kolkata, Kochi, Mumbai, Bangalore, Pune and Hyderabad.

Latest report indicates marginal decrease in crime rate at 0. 56 % but specific crimes increased. Cases of rape increased 1.1 %. There was surge of kidnapping and abduction 5.1 %. Higher crime rate was found in urban area as compared to the rural area. In 2024 crime rate is445.9 per lakh population starting from theft, robbery, to other crimes..

5. Present Homes not a solution in Place of Reformatory Schools

The position of our country at international level records a significant status on children. India is the home of the 19% population of the world. More than one third of the population are children. Considering the juvenile delinquency being attracted to crimes more in present days, it becomes to learn the institution and systems of past 150 years, in British India and the past law. Present classification of juveniles is of two types, male and female. This is categorized in two way, CICWL which means child in conflict with law and other one is CINOCAP which is child in need of care and protection. Child in conflict of law is sent to observation homes meant for temporary reception of juveniles during pendency of inquiry, Special homes are provisions for reception and rehabilitation of juveniles by juvenile justice board on conclusion of inquiry. For CINOCAP the homes are children home for adoption and foster care. In addition are after care hostel and shelter homes. There are more than 815 juvenile homes Police role at state level is the role of inspector general of police dealing juveniles. At the district level is special juvenile police unit SJPU under superintendent of police and at thana level child welfare officer. Total 815 homes in the country are being assisted under integrated child protected schemes, ICPS OF THE GOVERNMENT OF INDIA. Juvenile justice (care and protection) act 2000 of the children provides establishment of children by the state government. They may associate voluntary organization in the process. Under ICPS scheme of India financial help is given by the ministry of child and women development as approved in 2009-10 act. The homes state wise data say Andhra 102 homes, Assam 7, Bihar 14, Chhattisgarh 13, Gujarat 57, Haryana 12, Himachal 22, Jharkhand 16, Karnataka 76, Kerala 28, Madhya Pradesh 24, Maharashtra 91, Manipur 13, Meghalaya 18, Mizoram 4, Orissa 29. Punjab 15, Rajasthan 63, Tamil Nadu 42, Sikkim 5, Tripura 11 Uttar Pradesh 67, west Bengal 55 Delhi 25, Pondicherry 6 The objective of juvenile shelter homes was to protect, rehabilitate the juvenile delinquents. There are no definite locations of the homes as illustration where a delinquent is shown as reformed and rehabilitated. Reports in newspaper like Times of India has noted that the homes are not registered in major numbers as desired in section 34 (3) of the juvenile justice board act 2006.Adversely the children are being kept in home in bad condition like inhuman manner for which they are forced to leave the homes. It ED IN NEWS paper in 2016 one HIV juvenile was sexually assaulted by security guard in Alipur government run Ashiana home. In Haryana a home without license raped a minor girl for which police took them to custody. Since caretaker and owners sexually harassed minors, a committee formed by the Haryana government to enquire into cases were

99

formed. No congenial atmosphere of stay existed in several homes. There are several study reports from enquiry teams on shabby atmosphere including bad food, lack of medical facility, no recreation and education. Similar investigation in Assam after continuous harassment of sex to children in such homes, a report from Asian center of human rights defined shelter homes as hell holes of our nation. This does not give any effect on offender children for reformation, not even regret for crimes done by them. They even did not think of future rehabilitation or to become civil persons in society. Juvenile justice act 2000 being revised adopted minor amendments in which states should adopt measures for juvenile justice act despite federal act passed in parliament. The examination from residents of homes remarked that they do not get better foods nor scope of education. They also stated that their family income is also not good. It would be proper to understand performances of juvenile homes through various committee reports and more accuracy through Audit reports if any. Normally it is difficult to get audit reports as government policy to associate voluntary organizations. Pratichi institute located at Salt Lake; Kolkata took a survey in west Bengal on performances of juvenile homes of west Bengal. The report of 2014 reported some high lights. They found that 50% of children staying in juvenile homes had their family, parents, sibling with them. Factors of their stay was poverty and lack of educational facility with them. For above two factors, the children were forced to undergo for act under conflict of law. Children under conflict of law had no schooling facility, no
100

vocational training, no content with outer world. They were anxious for their future. Vocational training were irregular there and supported by NGOS.40 % CHILDREN IN government homes and 33% from NGO homes had desired new skills for their future living .in 67% of government homes no medical facilities was available and homes managed by NGO had only 50 % medical facility.50 % boys got cigarettes, alcohol on way to courts and 20 % by near and dear ones .Even in government run homes, there was no restoration of staffs and so also staffs were deficient in NGO run homes .inmates showed concerns on lack of education and medical facilities and there was no standard infra structures for homes .Over all the objective of reformation and rehabilitation of juvenile children are not addressed by this methodology as per the survey reports of west Bengal as made by experts undertaking the studies in this issues. Audit report ending 31st march 2015 on working of juvenile homes of Rajasthan maintained either by governments itself or in association with voluntary organizations has highlighted many facts on the matter .The report mentioned that state government failed to identify children in need of care and protection but adults in age group of 18 to 27 years were found admitted in juvenile observation homes .Homes were found only at divisional headquarters but not all districts .Infrastructure like dormitories, bath room ,dining hall ,library rooms etc. were inadequate .In checked homes nutritional food and clothing's were in adequate.8 government homes were providing 87 to 94% school education to children but not provided in such 2

101

homes. No vocational training was provided in any of the test checked homes. Integrated child protection scheme ICPS was though to provide grants to the observation homes in the child care programs. Referred children to child welfare committee sent them to NGO and children with conflict of law were sent to children observation homes by police department along with street children. The audit has objected to identification properly of children in need of care and protection violating guide line of ICPS 2009. Though sanction of 30 to 50 children in each home existed but less than 50 % children existed in government homes but two such homes were overcrowded in 2 governments homes. total homes were 10. Excess admission was noticed in NGO homes.121 adults in age group of 18 to27 and 2 adult in age group of 35 were admitted as per observation of concerned board. Reception unit of observation home was not working. There were non-separated children by category, gender and age. No separate children home and observation home s was found. The check was made at Baran, Bikaner, Jaipur etc. Despite provision to keep children in shelter homes, it was more than that at Jaipur. Total 55 children, boys 22 and girls 23 were residing more than one year in violation of JJ rules. Scrutiny of 13 test checked government homes showed poor infrastructure on dormitories, workshop, library etc. No medical facility maintained despite provision of medical record to be maintained under clause 45 of JJ rules, 2011.Education facility as required under clause 47 not given at Baran, Jhunjhuna homes. There is provision for action for not providing facilities
102

as issued circular of 2016, but no action is taken except NGO issued direction. After care program to be adopted by the government under section 44 of the act was not in action nor organizations were registered as required. Audit also expressed concern on lack of manpower management, lack of trainings of staffs and care not taken as directed by JJ board. The JJ board sits once in a year though there should be regular continuous sittings The grants allocated year wise by audit are as under on government homes and homes maintained by the NGO. (in crores) SI NO year allotment expenditure saving income

SI NO	year	allotment	expenditure	saving	income %
1	2010-11	10.74	7.47	3.27	30.44s
2	2011-12	9.92	6.70	3.22	32.46
3	2012-13	13.59	12.62	0.97	7.12s
4	2013-14	18.98	18.97	0.01	0,05
5	2014—15	36.16	29.22	6.94	19.19

government was said to send proposal to government of India for funds but state government did not send proposal for rationalization.

SI	District	no ofNGO	Allotment	Disbursement
1	Baran	2	1.30	0.41
2	Jaipur	14	4.84	1.15
3	jhunjhuna	1	0.08	-
4	Pali	1	0.15	-
5	swai madhopur	1	0.07	-

103

| 6 sikar | 2 | 0.90 | 0.28 |
| 7Tonk | 3 | 0.66 | 0.33 |

Pali, Sawai Madhopur, Jhunjhuna NGO not functioning but concerned DCPU are getting funds. Therefore, the so-called NGO, funds allocations, disbursement, maintenance are misuse of funds and objective contrary to Reformatory school provision as found closed which was regular government institutions of the four state, Bihar, West Bengal, Odisha and Asam under British rule and free India. The infrastructure still ill maintained better than any institution of India for juvenile offenders to be operated with accountability by the government and state.

For example, the latest report from Odisha as published in newspaper dated 2nd September 2024, it says increase in crimes of juveniles in heinous crimes. In Puri, increase of theft, murder, drug cases were in rise. there was involvement of 7 juveniles in two murder case on family conflicts. similarly recent theft at house of endowment commissioner, Bhubaneswar, Bargarh showed 5 juveniles out of 7 persons involved in theft. 865 juveniles were criminally connected as per report of NCRB 2022.Reformation home at Berhampur, Rourkela and Angul brought no correction of inmates in such hostels. The offenders are sent in homes for 3 years but after release no review is monitored on their corrections. Instances have come that habitual offenders utilize some of the children for their use. IT is said by expert that due to lack of stringent punishment rules on

juveniles, such increase is seen. There are
reports from Times of India dated 25 November,
2021 that at Delhi 10 juveniles are arrested
every month. There are reports of rising crimes
by juveniles at Chandigarh from 75 in 2021 into
151 in two years as reported in Indian Express,
NDTV released information on juvenile crimes
and reported that three minors were arrested for
extortion attempt for murder of 17 years and
after release from jail there is same attitude of
committing crimes. This shows no reformation
and rehabilitation. Juvenile justice act 2015 after
severe heinous crime of Nirbhaya murder at
Delhi followed with sex scandal speaks of care,
protection, treatment under constitution for two
category of children, 1. Children in conflict of
law,2. For care and protection of the children.
This law is not stringent on offence punishment
which is necessary for the realization. This
should have been followed with industrial
training in confinement with proper education as
was available in Reformatory school,
Hazaribagh which is at the stage of decay and
collapse created by British infrastructure with
plan and proper object of reformation in eastern
India for juveniles of four states.

There are cases in various states of India that
juvenile crimes has been gradually increasing
and the district wise data varies on the quantum
of offences differently considering the situations
in the states. The information on serious offense
of Odisha during September 2024 and
government information on the children home
have been placed in the next page.

105

Samaj 2nd Sept 2024

ଅପରାଧରେ ବଢ଼ୁଛି ନାବାଳକଙ୍କ ସଂପୃକ୍ତି

Report of inspection of child care institution of Odisha by national commission for child protection 2019. minister woman and child protection, India wrote to chief minister, Odisha on7 12 2018 in the matter., A study on 19 districts were taken up. I T observed that a portion of children are kept in the institution who would have been in families provided the officials in juvenile system could have been sensitized and individual care plan would have been drawn .There was need of implementation of JJ act 2015.Children from particular religion and faith are kept in one place .children were taught bible irrespective of their religious background in some homes .Apart from children under child care on JJ act, various institutions keep children in their facility like hostel of education , institutions. Including SC/ST and minorities.5 homes were recommended for closure for no infrastructure, home without registration, home without order of CWC, children influenced with religious conversion etc.21 homes were within in adequate security and many others lacunae. 13 homes were recommended for police enquiry. violation of provision 26JJcp act 2016., section 40 of jj rule2016 was noticed. no formation of management committee and children not produced before children welfare committee and violation of section 39 was seen. poor infrastructure, no segregation on age, gender etc. was seen. There were many deviations shown in the report. In Maharashtra a body in association with human right commission in its report of 2022 studying promotion, monitoring, upholding human rights for marginalized sections of

107

society gave a report after case study at Ulhaspur, thane of Mumbai. It said woman and children development department established network of children care institutions .The study there whether care home is equipped to mandate provision for children under JJ act 2015 and Maharashtra children care and protection rule 2002 showed change of nomenclature of state funds ,child with care missing, abandoned Bal graham ,children physically abused, child labor trafficked .No homes found proper to meet the requirements of the act .They noticed bad infrastructures in homes, door of toilet damaged ,toilets and wash rooms at distance from dormitory ,insanitary kitchens ,inadequate furniture ,no electricity for shortage of funds, lack of staff ,in sufficient capacity building ,lack of health, training facility, no doctor, no probation officer ,no practical training, MHRC report with Sahil Sanjay kadam and others as part of winter internship on 3rd January gave a report that do juveniles receive right care for development and rehabilitation and whether their fundamental rights are preserved or not. The visit of MHRC and kadam team on 24th January 2023 at juvenile court and juvenile home at Dongri, Mumbai found in British era, it was jail. FROM 1927 IT WAS CONVERTED to home which was biggest in Asia. capacity was 250. They visited David saloon school, Motunga having children in need of care and protection. They found carpentry done near entry which is unhygienic.no segregation of children in common rooms based on age and gender, offenders staying with other children, access to kitchen free, no discipline, use of common hall
108

for mess, dormitory un hygienic, no proper bed to sleep, window duct to bath room was not proper.

Protection Scheme (ICPS) along with year-wise financial assistance provided by the Government to each H each of the last three years and the current year is as following.

Sl. No.	Name of the State/UT	No. of Homes	Amount released (Rupees in Lakhs)			
			2010-11	2011-12	2012-13	2013-14 [up to 30.11.2013]
1.	Andhra Pradesh	105	553.50	1036.80	1995.94	704.83
2.	Arunachal Pradesh	1	-	-	2.75	1.38
3.	Assam	7	52.36	-	240.93	19.78
4.	Bihar	14	363.62	135.80	720.05	80.13
5.	Chhattisgarh	29	-	-	262.07	88.44
6.	Goa	-	-	-	-	-
7.	Gujarat	52	252.26	492.25	514.26	257.13
8.	Haryana	12	272.24	140.55	175.04	55.26
9.	Himachal Pradesh	22	-	156.77	-	31.53
10.	Jammu & Kashmir	-	-	-	-	-
11.	Jharkhand	15	-	150.37	-	55.88
12.	Karnataka	69	215.13	1031.66	914.49	1104.41
13.	Kerala	29	206.42	353.69		176.04
14.	Madhya Pradesh	44	-	91.44	376.78	138.77
15.	Maharashtra	60	3301.38	1061.73	636.94	213.87
16.	Manipur	12	26.43	174.11	197.42	98.71
17.	Meghalaya	18	29.44	133.62	204.58	102.39
18.	Mizoram	7	15.74	161.89	120.56	271.23
19.	Nagaland	19	-	116.90	305.82	342.39
20.	Orissa	124	295.36	310.81	292.17	137.87
21.	Punjab	15	-	231.13	-	62.34
22.	Rajasthan	14	-	846.91	1098.01	1577.76
23.	Sikkim	5	-	51.12	-	6.75
24.	Tamil Nadu	243	60.04	790.86	3868.22	1678.74
25.	Tripura	13	175.65	114.80	137.00	68.33
26.	Uttar Pradesh	64	-	900.46	1360.46	975.17
27.	Uttarakhand	15				74.03
28.	West Bengal	53	258.91	548.24	353.57	176.79
29.	Andaman & Nicobar Island	-	-	-	-	-
30.	Chandigarh	2	-	-	14.27	5.36
31.	Dadra & Nagar Haveli	-	-	-	-	-
32.	Daman & Diu	-	-	-	-	-
33.	Delhi	24	266.15	319.49	811.17	277.96
34.	Lakshadweep	-	-	-	-	-
35.	Puducherry	27	69.37	-	119.32	34.50
	Total	1210	6113.30	8951.10	15308.51	8754.86

6. Present Homes, Status, Impractical Solutions

The children's homes with highest numbers were from Tamil Nadu, Maharashtra, and Karnataka. Contrast to this least number of homes are from Arunachal Pradesh, Chandigarh, Sikkim. Observation homes are maximum in Maharashtra, Rajasthan, Madhya Pradesh. The combination homes not defined in JJ act 2015 are one or two in Andaman and Arunachal Pradesh. Special homes are from Karnataka, Andhra Pradesh and Rajasthan. Any other homes more in number are from Kerala, Andhra Pradesh and Jammu and Kashmir.

There are mandatory provisions under jj act 2015 about homes. They are compulsory registration, punitive measures for non-registration, scope of compliance in 6 months. The states having numbers and percentage registered under jj act were Andaman 10 (58.82%), Andhra Pradesh 138 (18.11 5%), Arunachal Pradesh 5 (62 %), Assam 62 (47. 33 %), Bihar 17 (20.24 %), Chandigarh 5 (31.25 %), Chhattisgarh 19. (15. 57 %), Delhi 70 (56 %), Goa 48 (68. 57 %), Gujrat 88 (52.07 %), Haryana 58 (73.42 %), Himachal Pradesh 5 (10. 87 %), Jammu and Kashmir 2 (0.55 %), Jharkhand (7. 09 %), Karnataka 147 (16.03 %), Kerala 219 (17. 63 %), Madhya Pradesh 44 (30.14 %), Maharashtra 652 (50. 78 %),

110

Manipur 29 (46. 77 %), Meghalaya 14 (16. 67 %), Mizoram 31 (63. 39 %), Nagaland 21 (31. 34 % 0, Odisha 263 (63 %). These are the government reports of 2018 from child and woman development departments. There must be the sufficient reasons of non-response in acceptance by the authority and though causes are not known but no future on application is decided in time. Therefore, we do not know the status of back ground in the matter.

This was the status on application for registered homes. But existence of unregistered CCI/ homes is also many. But applied for registered homes under JJ act are Andaman 3 (17. 65 %), Andhra Pradesh 50 (16. 56 %), Assam 4 (3.o5 %), Bihar 20 (23 .81 %), Chhattisgarh 9 (7. 38 %), Delhi 22 (17. 6 5), Goa 6 (8. 57 %), Gujarat 43 (25. 44 %), Haryana 6 (7.59 %), Himachal Pradesh 7(7 (5.22 %), Jammu and Kashmir 3 (0.89 %), Jharkhand 54 (42.52 %), Karnataka 228 (25. 03 %), Kerala 14 (1 .13%), Madhya Pradesh 14 (9. 59 %), Maharashtra 267 (20.59 %), Manipur 1 (1.61 %), Meghalaya 14 (16.67%), Mizoram 4 (8. 71%), Nagaland 1 (1. 49 %), Odisha 9 (2. 11 %), Pondicherry 65 (71. 43 %), Punjab 12 (16.44 %), though 22 exist, Rajasthan 25(9. 03%).

This shows that 65. 6 % c. c. homes were yet to be registered under juvenile justice act. 15.51 homes where registration has been applied for are beyond the act. In other schemes registered are 16. 53 %. These schemes cannot be under scanner of the legislation and their status cannot be ascertained. The data shows only 32. 03 % homes registered under JJ act. The registered

111

home maximum is in Sikkim 96 %., Haryana 58 (73. 42%), Goa 48 (69%) and lower status are in Jammu and Kashmir, Himachal Pradesh and Jharkhand.

About percentage of CCI oblique homes linked with outside professionals' oblique institutions for various services indicate Andaman 11.8 for vocational training whereas Andhra Pradesh has 26% linkage on vocational trainings.

Assam has 24.4 but Bihar has only 4%. It is somehow better at Chandigarh 75.0 but in Chhattisgarh only 23.8. In Delhi, 44.0 but in Goa 65.7. Gujarat has 42.0, Haryana 58.2, Himachal 13.0, J&K 6.9, Jharkhand 26.0, Karnataka 30.3, Kerala 23.6, Madhya Pradesh 25.3, Maharashtra 24.0, Manipur 33.9, Meghalaya 31.0, Mizoram 28.3, Nagaland 26.9, Odisha 30.7, Punjab 35.6, Rajasthan 48.4, Tamil Nadu 29.4, Telangana 21.1, Uttar Pradesh 34.1, Uttarakhand 37.5, West Bengal 57.5. On an average at national level linkage with outside was only 27.8% for vocational training. Linkage of states of Tamil Nadu, Odisha, Maharashtra, Jharkhand was between 16-10% only without outside institutions for profession.

Education by CCI homes arranged inside the homes or with outside agencies, the highest percentage was failed in CCI oblique homes of some states like Chandigarh 93%, Pondicherry 89% and Goa 79%. The minimum status of education arranged by homes was seen in Himachal Pradesh, J&K and Andaman. The good states in arranging life skills or issued based workshops in CCI oblique homes were seen in Haryana, Goa and New Delhi.

Percentage of NGO run CCI oblique homes having linkage with external institutions for restoration and rehabilitation of children showed Mizoram 81.8, Delhi 77.6, West Bengal 74.9, Tamil Nadu 73.2, Madhya Pradesh 72.6, Sikkim 72.2, Maharashtra 71.1, Meghalaya 67.7, Rajasthan 67.5, Odisha 67.2, Goa 65.2, Haryana 64.7, Gujarat 61.1, Punjab 61.0, Tripura 57.6, Karnataka 50.7, Chhattisgarh 44.4, Manipur 43.6, Assam 34.4, Bihar 26.3, Jharkhand 24.9, Kerala 21.0, Uttarakhand 20.5, Himachal Pradesh 5.3, J&K 2.1.

It is seen that major percentage of above homes in the country lack the linkage to the services or do not have provision of their own. Therefore, this is proved that homes have not taken homes for services of rehabilitation, training, education etc. at their own violating JJ act. The homes do not have facility, fund, knowledge for services to contact agencies.

The contrast was the facility in reformatory school, Hazaribagh having own workshops, school, skill training, medical facilities, diploma institute, teacher's training institute, industrial training institute, good fencing, good playground, gymnastics center, vocational training, recreation and a protected boundary which are under process of decay and destruction due to lack of sincerity of the government nor people have knowledge of such respective institutions. Regarding the present facilities, in elimination of reformatory act and adoption of acts after independence from 1960, there were deficiencies of proper education, training, future of the prisoners. Present cases are

113

1. Institutional care as per JJ act 2015, not covered in CCI oblique homes run by NGO or government as was available in reformatory school, Hazaribagh. Under this act having all infrastructure facilities.
2. No implementation of Mission Vatsalya or vocational, educational and other programs by state or center.

A detailed study and number of investigations as reported by many researchers in matter of deficiencies are noted below:
Large number of homes don't have dormitories.
Education, safety, privacy infrastructure in the compound not available.
Improvement in running water, drinking water necessary.
Proper drainage and garbage removal.
Safety not provided.
Production before SWC oblique JJB initially was only 49.9%.
No financial transparency was seen in the management.
50% of audit report submitted and many homes not audited.
Social audit report on an average was 7% (Meghalaya 31%)
Rationalization of availability of CCI homes based on district needs to be registered.
Assessment of homes not done under JJ act.
Provision of place of safety not guaranted.
Child protection policy not assured

There are no statutory committees.
Separation homes based on JJ act not arranged.

These are due to lack of proper policy by the government and the legislation is improper. The government involvement and their financial responsibilities in correction of future of juvenile is more or less very poor. In reformatory school Hazaribagh then, 4 states: Bihar, West Bengal, Assam, Odisha were together taking the financial responsibility for juveniles with training and education by then respective governments of the states.

A study on juvenile justice, care and protection of children act, 2000 closed and Tamil Nadu justice act 2001 by G. Vigneshwari, Dr. A. Thaanapan has focused on causes for juvenile delequency and majors of for children in conflict of law. The causes are the parent-child relationships, violence on computer, laptop, cell phones, T.V programs, movies etc. The law is revived as per UN convections 1989 for which 1986 laws were changed. Prisoners as juveniles below age of 18 under section 27 of act IX 1894 stated to keep them separated from adult prisoners. Females will be kept in female wards. The apprentice act and reformatory act was made to trick them separately than others. The revised act now kept them different from adult jails, adult courts and police and were kept under guidance of juvenile courts, remand homes, probation certified school. This approach for rehabilitation, formation of child welfare committee, inquiries, children home, inspection of children home, observation home after care organization etc. was the considerable steps in implementation of the acts for amendment of the minors as offenders with liberalized policies taking into consideration the policies adopted by UN in year 1986.

The study at Roya Puram showed overcrowding in homes from 250-850. Girls at KEELY 275 in government observation homes against provision of sixty boys and girls. There is an inflow and outflow of children. Funds were private collections to give food, maintain toilets, health etc. In conclusion it was said the rehabilitation was of juvenile was necessary and could not be solved by such homes.

The ministry of women and children development, government of India said to bring amendments in 2011 consulting stakeholders. A draft bill is pending before the ministry of law and placed in web side of women and children development in June 2014. No amendments, no financial assistance and specification of government control homes with infrastructure for vocational training, education could come up by the government. So is the state of affair in different states of the country. The law from 1960 by parliament and thereafter through various amendments of acts from time to time is a liberal, impractical and unnatural consideration in reformation or rehabilitation of the juvenile delinquents.

While dealing with the juvenile delinquents in India, by Dr. Ramesh Kumar Bharadwaj or Kurukshetra University the following recommendations were made:

1. Provision of JJ act should be adopted properly, strictly
2. Despite provision of special police unit, they do not handle cases properly.
3. Social worker should council students and parents
4. Parents, family members should be educated for proper responsibility.
5. Recreation program in communities should be arranged at leisure time.
6. Community should be made of legislation on juveniles.
7. The role of voluntary organization in the matter be affected.
8. Motivation by government for rehabilitation scheme must be mandatory.

Though JJ act 2015 transfers 16–18-year-old children to adult criminal courts for heinous crimes considering Nirbhaya Case 2012, but power rests with JJ board to refer which court whether adult or children will be dealt. On recommendation of jail community, 1919-20, children act 1920 established children's court. After independence, children act 1960 prohibited police or jail for children within this provision. As per supreme court in Sheela Barse 1983 it stated that cut off age differently in states be removed for equality. Then 1996 act of parliament concept of child in state of juvenile brought a change though adopted the same in 1960. Girl up to 18 and boys up to 16 were kept at child juveniles.

The gang rape of Jyoti Pandey (Nirbhaya) highlighted of involvement of 17-year-old boy in sex matter which brought some changes in age matter for juveniles by the parliament. In criminal amendment act 2013, media highlighted juvenile rights though NCRB said average in increase of juvenile crime. 2015 act accepted offenses up to 18 years as child offense or offense by minor.

Such children will be under JJ board with one justice and two social persons added with child welfare committees. Under section 6, person crossing 18 years is apprehended of doing crimes prior to 18 years but will be child. But without school certificate, age determination is subject of hard task by the authority in deciding the offense and this has been subjected to various conflicts in supreme court and other courts where offenders have been taking advantages. Though age being critical factor, many were released by courts on the issue despite offenses. For serious crimes, JJB and condition of child, it may pass order for action or may refer children court which will decide to try it as an adult or otherwise. For cases above 21 years the annual review or monitoring will be taken by children court for release. This is provision for 16–18-year aged child. Before the act of 2015 could have been passed, genesis of crimes

118

and history could have been taken into consideration in formulation of the law of the country which would have provided many more amendments and improvements in the laws framed by the parliament and various states. Unfortunately, the lawmakers as well as the legislatures have not gone to the basic concept of the Indian system and made laws for juveniles with a policy of liberty and relaxation without punitive, reformative and rehabilitation policies, so that, the offenders competing their tenure for offense could have joined civil societies and could have also employment to maintain their livelihood.

As per NCRB, 56031 boys of sixteen-18-year-old age were convicted against girls numbering 333 only. This shows that the boys are more involved in offense as juveniles as compared to girls.

The international status accepted by India with liberalization in billing juvenile laws in India since 1960 was not adequate and pull off laxity. There is improvement in the act of juvenile justice care and protection 2015 but country legislation should have thought of increasing trend of juvenile crimes in India and population of the country as a whole. The USA has not responded to UN laws and has its own law on juveniles. Somalia and South Sudan at later stage have responded to UN laws. There are several global rankings that majors the wellbeing of juveniles including youth development index but that is not index for India being highly population country. Belgium records

119

least juvenile crimes but justice system is caused of priority there. UK law of 1908 is remand homes under criminal justice act are for training or reformation. Portugal and Spain are better ranked countries. When Belgium scores 81.6% being ranked first, India scored 64% with UK 73%, Japan 145%, even Sri Lanka 130%. Therefore, the justice law should be more practical and we'll need to understand the factors of juvenile crimes and trend of increase or decrease of juvenile crimes. In this perspective, we may discuss the trends. UK is going towards tougher policy than rehabilitation. In India, only age factor is main thrust but not gravity and severity of crime with intention to overcome the same. First juvenile court in US was 1899 in Cooke country, Illinois. The reform in between 1970-1985 on juvenile policy where on the criminalization and the institutionalization. Presently, slogan of adult crimes is accepted in 38 states with upper age of juvenile being 17 years.

In billing policies, we have to see trends of crimes, rising or diminishing. Offenses on IPC crimes category like affecting human body and miscellaneous crimes increase from 2007-2011. But offense on property decrease from 2017-2020. Which again increase 2021. There is rising trend on children related acts from 2017 which is 933 (2018, 1318), 2019 (1763), 2020 (1904), 2021 (2446). There is similar increase in liquor and narcotic drugs related act from 803 to 1466 from 2017 (22021).

Considerable increase in arms/explosive related acts from 272 to 289 in between a period of in the matters of juveniles. There is also increasing trend on theft, murder, robbery etc.

In gender of the juvenile apprehended between 2017-2021, the boys were 99% girls 1% and transgender 0%. The boys apprehended under IPC from 2017-2021 where from 40155-37092 with girls from 265-350.

Total incidence, percentage and the rate of juvenile crimes from 2017-2021 where 0.67 to 0.5%. Crime rate was 7.527%, incidence of juvenile crime was 33606 to 31170.

Present days, child offense are also more with murders and sexual harassment which are increasing in India and youths are very casual in the habits and the motives to continue with above offenses.

India is home to 305 million children aged 6+18 years representing 43% population. 39 (1) article of constitution speaks protection of children. The criminal responsibility as per age varies in world countries. In 1843 Lord Cornwallis established ragged school for reformed child. 1850 came apprentice act as juvenile legislation for 10-18 years children wherein they had to go vocational training as a reformation process. IPC 1860 bisection 82, 83, fixed juvenile court. CRPC 1861-1898 by section 298, 399, 562 gave separate trails below 15 years age in reformatory school act 18i76. Detention period was from 2-7 years. Jail committee 1919-1920 said separate institution and separate jails for juveniles. Madras children act 1920, followed by west Bengal and Bombay 1922 and 1924 recommended for separate jail for juveniles, following England law 1908. Post-independence act are 1960, 1986, 2000, 2015 children act of JJ (KRN) protection of children act. It may be reiterated that juvenile justice act 1986 was due to Sheela Barse KS decided by supreme court for a uniform law with the country and parliament of India enforced a same by article 250 accepting international obligation having signed in 1989. The act 2000 was important making below 18 years as juvenile due to supreme court order King Amit Das vs. Bihar (AIR 2000), Umesh Chandra vs Rajasthan (AIR 1982) Pratap Singh vs Jharkhand (AIR 2005) while determining the date of offense as juvenility as no clarity in law was made by the lawmakers and matter remained as a conflict. Finally in 2015, law after Nirbhaya case of Delhi made 16-18 years age as an adult to be punished for heinous crimes with 7 years of imprisonment. JJB will decide if child be treated as adult or minor. Looking to child condition and the same decision has to be finalized within a period 3 months. Recently, in Khan vs Maharashtra, 17-year child murdered 3 years old, remained in JJ system and 16-year-old charged of murder to 7-year-old child was charged as adult. The percentage of juvenile convicted was 87% in 2018. Supreme court on crime of rape and murder now said that it can't be conceived that consequences are not known by culprits. Victim has right of justice in law. The JJB has to consider to treat as adult on heinous crimes. Tendency of cases before JJB are more in number. By the end of 2018, 41709 cases were pending before the juvenile justice board.

Obviously the functioning of the JJB needs a serious discussion so far implementation of juvenile justice board act of 2015 are concerned. The earlier acts of 1960 and afterwards though has been modified properly through the parliament adopting 2015 juvenile justice act, yet all these acts and its actions must be viewed in context of reformatory act adopted by British government and the institution they built up in Hazaribagh, Yerwada as well as Chingleput of Madras. Unless you do not give facilities of good infrastructure and training we cannot expect more reformation or rehabilitation in correction of the juveniles.

7. Rising Trends in Juvenile Crimes, Matter of Concern

The Juvenile delinquency in practical term is a continuous evil of the society perpetuating since long. Its historical remedy in 19th century created a base of mapping of its intensity worldwide. Considering present day, mechanical and unethical life in society due to modernization and self-sicker attitude, there is a gradual decay of value in life style and juveniles are not separate than that. The anxiety to seek more in civil society avoiding honesty, integrity and reputation is a growing trend among people. No respect for police, judicial system, people society is the cause of crimes as the system sometimes fails in curbing criminality, terrorism, theft, robbery, sexual abnormality, trafficking, family disorder, rough driving, property disputes etc. The recommendations on category of offense in a detention institute are indicators of crimes and they differ. This is not applicable to many countries for the type of offenses as per countries suitability. Therefore, institutes differ as per category of offense and crimes. UN says that categories of offenses maybe amended as per suitability of the particular country. They say to disaggregate indicators by the type of institutions where the child is held. Recommended category can be adjusted as needed based on country's situation in type of detention institution are police station cells, juvenile detention policy, juvenile rehabilitation facility/school, prison (detention facilities, housing) for both children and adults even if separated.

While taking into consideration the reformation and rehabilitation of the delinquents after independence in our country started from 1966 as a policy in parliament. No laws were enacted by the center or state to take responsibility for the amendments by the governments as was taken by the Britishers investing government expenditures through establishing reformatory schools. Hazaribagh Reformatory School can be cited as the best example which had the infrastructure built by the Britishers resembling British structures and was also called Gora Jail during first world war period in which foreign prisoners were accommodated. There is a building Rani Bungalow named perhaps by a reputed queen which could not be discovered due to lack of available evidence. The juvenile delinquents of four eastern states, Bihar, Bengal, Odisha, Assam were sent here for reformation and rehabilitation through trainings in a big workshop created by Britishers and maintained by expenditure of these states. Bihar government was controlling this system under the avail of education department. Director of public instruction of these states were meeting in a year to have a relook or to meet the deficiency in development through education, vocational training, agriculture training as explained in the first chapter.

125

Such a big infrastructure with workshops, agricultural farms, diploma institute, teacher's training institute, industrial training institute, were closed due to state government of Bihar opening Indira Girls Residential School where all the institutions infrastructure old buildings died and large infrastructure was not utilized due to closure of the workshop and workshop, schools, farms etc. it may be mentioned that trend delinquents were being employed by Tata Steel and other institutions after these trend delinquents released from the reformatory school on completion of their tenure of captivity. The Hazaribagh Reformatory School was very old institution where purified water connections was made available through lake no. 4 through purified station maintained and operated by Coal by then. Subsequently, the water connection was made available from Chadwa Dam in which water is stored for the whole district for supply to the residents. A special tank stored with water was made, it was managed by the state government organization deploying their staffs for regular supply of water to reformatory school, staff quarters and training institutes. Large number of sweepers were employed for clearance of waste material and night soil from the dormitories and residential quarters as well as staff quarters made in the colony for working staffs of the reformatory schools. Similarly, there was a housing arrangement for working sweepers in a separate colony for residence of the working staff's family of the sweepers who were rendering services in the reformatory schools.

Every hospital under a government doctor deputed by Bihar government with compounder, dresser, pharmacist and other assisting staffs were available for 24-hour services which were useful for the inmates as well as staffs of the reformatory school. A big hospital building inside the compound of the school was built where minor surgeries and medicinal treatments were being given to the inmates and staffs. As per the act civil surgeon of the district was also connected with the institution who used to make frequent visits to the school to look after the medical facilities being operated in institutes. It may be mentioned that Dr. Panna Lal, Dr. Mehra and other civil servants were keenly involved and after them also the civil surgeon were giving their services.

Entry gate of Reformatory School.

A portion of dormitory at first floor in the school
and workshop on the ground floor. Altogether
five portions were there.

Main entry corridor of the school. There were other corridors as well.

Entry road near lake number 3 to go to
reformatory school.

131

In similar manner there was a reformatory school at Yerwada, Pune close to central jail campus. The location of reformatory school and Yerwada, Pune was same near my campus of the central jail and adult prison jail at Pune. This school was meant for juveniles from various states of western India as was reformatory school Hazaribagh where inmates from 4 eastern states of India like Bihar, Bengal, Odisha, Assam were being sent for reformation of the juveniles.

The author made visits to the present setup and status at Yerwada, Pune of the institute and could know that presently the old campus is under control of JJB now called Bal Grih. 24 inmates who were juveniles are housed there temporarily and under direction of juvenile board. They are housed for 3-4 months. Regular counseling of crime control, anger management, are done by invited social workers. Every month necessary arrangements are followed as per the instruction of the JJB. Probation officer, administrative officer, police and few other staffs are available in the institution. If court feels sending juvenile to adult courts they recommend for the same. School dress, food, water, ration, are freely provided to the inmates. Physical training classes, yoga, computer training, prayer and music classes etc. are being arranged for the temporary juveniles. There is also provision for career counseling and parent counseling. Now gymnasium is also developed. Earlier when it was a reformatory school, 4-5

132

dormitories were available and recently 4 new
dormitories have been created for stay of these
temporary juvenile delinquents. Some teachers
are engaged for imparting education program in
the building. There is a superintendent of the Bal
Grih but the judicial magistrate officiates in the
office during entry of the Bal Grih and is the
control authority as per the provision of the act
operating in Maharashtra State. The entry gate is
the same of the old reformatory school. The
system is half police guidance and half
education counseling programs. In addition,
some training on carpentry, tin, developed there
are being given to these inmates. There is a band
coaching program to the inmates. There is a
regular prayer program being conducted in the
Bal Grih campus.

Entry gate of old reformatory school, now Bal
Grih, Yerwada.

Entry nomenclature of the present gate.

Old buildings in front of gate in damaged
condition.

The reformation of act and government
institutions with accountability adopted and
institution like reformatory school should be
adopted to avoid 91% of management of homes
run by the NGOs. The laxity in homes and
superficial accountability made by policymakers
and adopted by NGOs haven't given though of
reality in the process of correction of juveniles.
To overcome the position, it will be necessary to
draw court rulings also. Madhya Pradesh high
court has published in September 2024 observe
that juveniles are treated too leniently in the
country. Legislature has still not learnt any
lessons from horrors of Nirbhaya. This was said
by the justice Subodh Abhayankar upholding the
conviction of a juvenile for rape of 4-year-old
girl.

Allahabad high court as per report published in 2022 denying bail to a juvenile who raped a 8 year old girl court said for counseling and said he needs to be extended services of reformatory and rehabilitative nature.

A study published up I probono revealed that between 2016 to 2021, at least 9681 children in conflict of law were transferred from prisons to child care institutions. In August 2024 updated report in a rare instance, Delhi court has sentenced a child in conflict of law (CCL) to life for raping and murdering 5-year-old girl in 2017.

JJB said that boy then 16-year-old should be tried as an adult in POCSO court. Bombay high court have asked to ensure juvenile unit at every police station.

The number of approaches in courts to get relaxation stressing the age factor as a juveniles allowed criminals to escape. The function of JJB is also not so fertile in resolving the issue and the justice system was forced to be ill-named.

We may refer recent ported publication in times of India (10th October 2024), Pune in the working of system of JJB placed here.

The said news confirms that state government of Maharashtra terminated the services of two members of JJB for misuse of powers. A 17-year-old boy driving the car had killed two software engineers on May 19th 2024. He was the son of influential businessman and a builder. There was so much leniency and rules of JJ act was violated by the justice. It may be that the parents were very influential persons and might have influenced the members of JJB who gave the bail to the offender despite several hue and cry in the media of the severe nature of this case and the manner he was given the bail. Finally, the Maharashtra government made an inquiry committee and after completion of inquiry the two members were terminated after the recommendation of the state government and considering the finding of the committee. So, it is not out of way to mention that the JJB direction in juvenile cases are appropriate and the law framed by the legislature for JJB is a very lenient and poor act.

Thus, the powers conferred to officials as well as others like NGOs who claim to build up bases in the name of juvenile reformation are free to move in their personal motive with no audit, no accountability and no objective. The government should not forget that it is accountable under law to deal with juvenile policies for reformation and rehabilitation with perfection for the juveniles so that the they can join as a member of the civil society.

138

Additionally, it will be proper to illustrate that nowadays the juveniles are adopting various new methods in the pattern of crimes, more particularly due to new trend of cybercrimes as well as for the introduction of information technology. Therefore, the delinquent or offenders can't be treated as innocent while adopting various methodologies. The legislation should not ignore this crisis. Some of the methodologies as published for public consumption is being cited for memory of the readers.

The report of Times of India 6th October 2024 states 3 minors during play in premises of housing society approached victim and took him aside, forcibly made him watch obscene films on a mobile phone followed with sexual act. The mobile phone is a tool for minors in offense. The news clip is annexed herewith:

Kondawa police produced the boys before the JJB in case of sexual assault of 5-year-old boy. The board went on to order the trios detention in an observation home following a complain case lodged by 28-year-old mother with the police in the crime committed here. This also is very painful on the motive of crimes with so less aged children and is a matter of discussion.

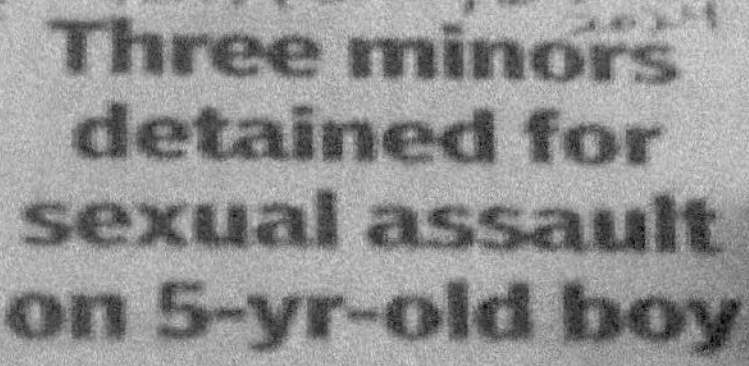

Three minors detained for sexual assault on 5-yr-old boy

Asseem Shaikh
@timesofindia.com

Pune: Three minor boys were detained on Friday in the Kondhwa area on the charge of sexually assaulting a five-year-old boy between Aug and Sept this year.

The Kondhwa police produced the boys before the Juvenile Justice Board. The board went on to order the trio's detention in an observation home on Friday.

The incident came to light after the victim's 28-year-old mother lodged a complaint with the police, following which an FIR under the Protection of Children from Sexual Offences Act was registered immediately.

A police officer told **TOI** that the boy was playing with many of his friends on the premises of a housing society. It was then that the three minors, aged 10, 11 and 13 years, approached him. They took him aside and forcibly made him watch obscene films on a mobile phone.

Later, the trio sexually assaulted the five-year-old boy and misbehaved with him on numerous other occasions. Their persistent pursuing scared the boy, who decided to confide in his mother.

The officer said the little boy complained to his mother about the regular harassment that he was facing. The mother decided to take action against her son's tormentors. The police took serious cognisan-

Another information of Mahoba, Uttar Pradesh for placing a cement pillar on a railway track on Jhansi Prayagraj Road route was done by minor. Passenger track was on a way to Prayagraj when loco pilot spotted the pillar on the track near Raibhara village. A teen walking animal in the field near the track confessed during interrogation that he placed pillar on the track. Police registered case under section 327. Earlier on September 2022, a five-liter empty gas cylinder was placed at Kanpur Prempur railway station track. On September 16th a wooden log was lying on the railway track between Gajipur ghat and Gajipur city railway station. The news item of Times of India September 30th of 2024 is being cited.

Now a serious concern has developed on involvement of children being used by many elders who are in constant habit of placing the explosive materials in the railway track so that the trains and passengers suffer. This has been growing in fast manner creating anxieties as the life of people travelling through trains has been put in risk. There are several cases but we are citing in the next page one of the reported items for the readers.

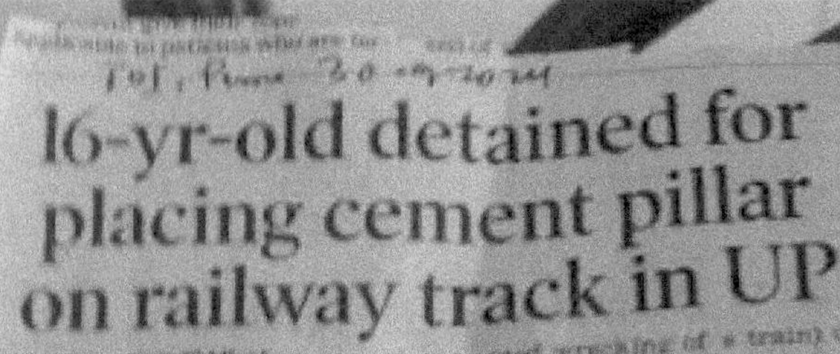

16-yr-old detained for placing cement pillar on railway track in UP

Photograph of the article placed in the railway track, September 30th, 2024.
Peculiar offenses are coming up adopted by minors. 13-year-old boy sent a hoax bomb threat e-mail which led to a Delhi-Toronto flight being rescheduled on June 4th. No less than 301 passengers and 16 crew members were made to disembark and their aircraft was diverted to the isolation bay for security check. The news published in Times of India on June 12th, 2024

142

established the fact and was painful as well as surprising for involvement of minors for such risky job or terrorizing the passengers. Such concept definitely confirms the present trend of delinquency that minors are not at all fearing in creating public horror.

The T.V news channel of OTV and Kanak News T.V of Odisha published 12 hoax bomb cases for various aircrafts on 16th October 2024 which created terror and was taken with surprise. This consideration cannot be accepted as an ideal effort, action or consideration. Obviously, this is negative trend which the minors are adopting and can be said to be very notorious for the society which needs complete correction through stringent policies of law.

More concern is now hoax emails cases adopted by children both in air route as well as railway route. Recently in the last 1 month a continuous email hoax message was conveyed to various airlines in India. This has been a terror activity which puts to the officers of the air route as well as railway route to be cautious and to go with anxieties. The enquiry by the police in such types of hoax emails has been found many as false ones but the way of functioning in which juveniles are also included are matters of worry. Therefore the crimes are many fold and are being built up in various manners in India. This needs settlement either through reformation or a good punishment. All the time things cannot be taken in casual manner in the nation on offences.

143

News item June 12 2022.

Similarly unacceptable action of a father who is a professor in IIT Roorkee did sexual offense against his son. Indian society are not appreciating this order behavior of individuals because our society is very much concerned on civil acts of society and can never appreciate action of bad conduct. Either in the family or in the society. The court punished professor for inappropriate action against the son. FIR was launched by the police in 2017 under section 377 (unnatural sex) of the IPC and the POCSO act. This information is unexpected and society cannot accept as our culture and traditions are based on ethical values which individuals adopt. Therefore, minors' involvement being ignorant or simple is also matter of worry which the civilized society has started to adopt as maybe evident from the publication made in July 31st 2024 in the ToI newspaper.

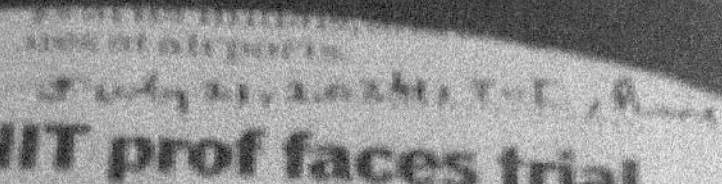

IIT prof faces trial for 'sex crimes' against minor son

Dehradun: An IIT-Roorkee professor will face trial for alleged sexual offences against his son following the dismissal of his petitions by the Uttarakhand high court. The court upheld a family court's order directing him to pay his wife and son monthly maintenance of Rs 45,000 and supported earlier allegations of inappropriate acts against his son.

The incidents occurred between 2010 and 2013 when the professor was working in Germany, and between 2015 and 2017, when he was employed at IIT-Roorkee. The professor, who has taught at prestigious institutes in India and abroad, was married in 2010. His wife accused him of forcing her into unnatural sex and showing pornographic content to their minor son. An FIR was lodged in 2017 under Section 377 (unnatural sex) of the IPC and the Pocso Act. TNN

As per reports of 4th October, two minors at Delhi gunned down Unani doctor. Two shooters who were minors entered hospital posing as patients. One was treated for a purported foot injury and entered the cabin of the doctor and shot him in the head. The two fled on a

146

motorcycle. The breakthrough came when police found CCTV footage showing the minor shoot Akhtar, flash a victory sign and flee the hospital on the motorcycle. The cops checked the minors in Instagram accounts where he posted a photo of himself, posing with pistol, boasting "first murder of 2024". This came in the newspaper in ToI 4th October 2024. We may consider the matter seriously on the audacity and objective of the minors of such daring risk calculated actions adopted by them for murder and the plea taken of foot injury on false shoot ground. This objective among minors has now become very adverse for the society as how they dared to enter as a patient and malign the doctor and shoot him dead. Can anyone today conceive that the present law which such types of culprits and offenders can show leniency in giving punishment in the name of JJB, counseling by psychologists and social people. This cannot be taken as an act of counseling as the action of the minors are just like adult offenders which is bad for Indian social society. Therefore, there is a need for reconsideration in legislation without leniency for which the court has also observed.

4TH October 2024 article.

A standard XII student of a prominent college in Baramati College was stabbed to death by two friends studying in the same institute before administrative building. The duo attacked the victims (17 years of age) with sickle and knife that they had hidden in their college bags. The police superintendent Pankaj Deshmukh said to media that they will request the JJB for permission to treat them as adult during trials. This action of the police could only come due to amendment of juvenile justice act 2015 after the Nirbhaya case that gives a scope for trial of offender in between age of 16-18 in adult court for heinous crimes. Earlier for a long time again the relaxation in punishment without stringent law in the name of counseling created a setback for which in present days the minors have been adopting very cruel and undisciplined way of life which is very painful for the society. The reported news in this case of creating injury in

148

the same college keeping the weapon in the bag
and use of sickle and knife obviously also
pushes a question on the college administration
and the institute that they are not in a position to
take individual observation of the students on
conduct and integrity which is also part of
education.

Two 17-yr-old students smuggle in sickle & knife into Baramati college, kill mate

Mihir.Tanksale
@timesofindia.com

Pune: A Std XII student of a prominent college in Baramati was stabbed to death by two friends studying in the same institute around Monday noon in front of its administrative building.

The duo attacked the victim, 17, with a sickle and a knife that they had hidden in their college bags. Police have detained one of the attackers, and are tracing the other student.

Pankaj Deshmukh, superintendent of police (Pune Rural), said, "The assailants involved in the murder are 17 years old. We will request the Juvenile Justice Board for permission to treat them as adults during trial."

Ganesh Biradar, additional superintendent of police, Pune Rural, told TOI: "Prima facie investigations revealed that the murder was the fallout of heated arguments between the deceased student and one of the suspects over a motorcycle."

> A police officer said one of the attackers was from Baramati. The other two students were, however, not natives of Baramati. The victim was staying in a hostel in the town

"The students had hidden a sickle and a knife inside their college bags and gained entry inside," Biradar said. After noticing the victim standing in front of the administrative building, they approached him and assaulted him with the sharp weapons, he added.

The incident created panic among other students on campus. "CCTV footage recovered from the college showed that after stabbing the victim, the duo started running away. Some people chased them and nabbed one of them. The other student fled," Biradar said.

▶Continued on P 5

150

Duo murder college mate in Baramati

▶ Continued from Page 1

After the police team reached the spot, they took the student into custody. "During questioning, the student claimed that he and the victim has been having some altercations for the past few days. The student also claimed that the victim had recently tried to hit him with a motorcycle. Following that incident also, they got into an argument," Biradar said.

The two students then hatched a plot to eliminate the victim and executed it on Monday, he added. Police added that one of the attackers is from Baramati, while the victim and the other student are not natives of Baramati. "We have informed the victim's parents," the officer said. On Sept 21, sub-divisional police officer Sudarshan Rathod conducted a meeting in the college about the country's laws and sexual offences. "The suspects and the deceased had at-

Minor stabbing with sickle and knife incident on October 1ˢᵗ.

Similarly 16 year old murdered a 17 year old minor and injured the latter friend in a knife attack following a dispute during Navaratra of 2024. As per Amrish Deshmukh, assisstant inspector who detained the teenager said 17 year old and the suspect accidentally met and had a

151

heated argument. The teenager asked the suspect to meet him near former's house. The suspect also arrived with knife. The 17 year old attacked the suspect with the billhook. However the suspect dodged it and assaulted the 17 year old faced with the knife. This has been reported in ToI 17th october 2024.

It may be mentioned that knife has been a casual tool for the minors to deal with it which earlier children were not in a position to speak on such tools because of social orders in our culture of the country. Such horrible operations adopted by minors have now become a matter of concern and the country's legislation and rulemaking body must give airy thinking on the matter as to why these minors have come up to this stage to stab with the help of a knife as a fashion and the punishment should be silent which are crimes of gravity.

Minor stabs teen & friend; detained

Mihir.Tanksale
@timesofindia.com

Pune: A 16-year-old murdered a 17-year-old and injured the latter's friend in a knife attack on Tuesday night following a dispute during Navaratra.

Assistant inspector Ambarish Deshmukh, who detained the teenager, said on Tuesday afternoon, the 17-year-old and the suspect accidentally met and had a heated argument. "The teenager asked the suspect to meet him near the former's house," he said.

The victim and his accomplice reached Nigdi on a motorcycle, carrying a billhook with them. The suspect also arrived with a knife. "The 17-year-old attacked the suspect with the billhook. However, the suspect dodged it and assaulted the 17-year-old in

The juveniles, children in low age are being raped. The victim and offenders have started the cases of sexual abuses which they should not have. The cases are rising. What may be the causes? There is no fear of law on society is not concerned in removal of misconducts of minors at low age. There is not government concern for
153

elimination of such practices. The police force not being independent are also having apathy to take up the issue. The governement policy to curb the crimes in this democratic setup to earn votes having many laxicities are matter of concern in the public life of India. In Joynagar of South Ferghana, West Bengal recently, a 9 year old girl's battered body was found in a ditch near her home. Villagers having no police action for perfunctory police action on complain protested in mass for no action. Police station was ransacked. It became because public mind was not happy with the protection or safeguard despite a dead body of the girl being available. Thereafter Mostakin Sardar, 19 years old was arrested who admitted of killing the girl. The girl's body was found with multiple injuries with tattered clothes. This is a crime of juvenile not seriously taken by the police. The news item contains rapes incident of Lakhimpur Kheri of Uttar Pradesh and a case involving Badodara. The photograph of news dated 6th october 2024 is being placed. Society must be concerned of the news and status of such type of cases and there must be conciousness in public life to check these crimes of juveniles. The government must realise the seriousness of the cases growing day to day among juveniles as indicated in the news placed below.

TIMES NATION, Pune

6th Oct 2024

Bengal villagers attack police after child's body found in ditch

9-Yr-Old's Kin Allege Rape, Cop Inaction

Monotosh Chakraborty | TNN

Joynagar (South 24 Parganas): A nine-year-old girl's battered body was found in a ditch near her home at Joynagar in Bengal's South 24 Parganas early Saturday, triggering a rampage by villagers who alleged "perfunctory" police response on a complaint since she went missing a previous day after leaving home for tuition. Her family alleged she was raped and murdered.

The protesters ransacked police outpost in Joynagar's Mahismari village, set it on fire and rained stones on the personnel, forcing the cops to run more than 1km to escape the fury that unfolded against the backdrop of nearly 2 months of agitations over rape and murder of a doctor in Kolkata's RG Kar hospital.

Earlier in the day, Mostakin, a 19-year-old resident of Mahismari village, was arrested on charges of murder. A class IV student. "He admitted to killing the girl but denied raping her. We are waiting for the post-mortem report," said Baruipur SDPO Rajanish Chandra Dhali.

The girl had left home for a place barely a kilo-metre away around 2pm on Friday and that was the last her family saw of her. "We lodged a complaint at Mahismari police outpost around 7pm but officials showed no urgency in either registering it or starting a search," said the girl's father. The girl's body — with multiple injury marks and tattered clothes — was found in the ditch around eight hours later in the wee hours of Saturday.

The protests started as day broke, with hundreds joining in as word spread.

Teen, bleeding and untreated, dies 14 days after rape in UP

A 14-year-old girl, who was brutally raped on Sept 20 in Lakhimpur Kheri, died at a hospital in Lucknow early on Saturday, reports **Kanwardeep Singh**. Police said the minor who had suffered excessive bleeding for days wasn't admitted to hospital by her family — neither did they report the matter to police — for almost 11 days after the assault, due to fear of social stigma.

ASP (Kheri) Pawan Gautam said that soon after the complaint on Oct 1, an FIR was registered under sections of rape and the Pocso Act against a local. "A police team is investigating the case, and they inspected the crime scene as well. The accused will be arrested soon," Gautam added.

A police officer said that on the day of the assault, the girl had gone to meet a relative. While returning home alone, the accused caught her at a secluded place and raped her after threatening her with a knife. "She then somehow reached home and narrated the ordeal to her parents. Since the accused lived in the neighbourhood, her family initially didn't register an FIR," the officer added. "However, when the girl's condition worsened due to excessive bleeding, the family took her to hospital but only on Oct 1, days after the brutal assault. She died during treatment."

16-year-old gang-raped, male friend attacked in Vadodara

A 16-year-old was allegedly gang-raped in the presence of her male friend in Vadodara late Friday night. The alleged assault took place in Bhayli, a developing suburb that now has no streetlights or CCTVs, compounding the challenges in tracking down the perpetrators.

Around midnight, five people on two bikes spotted the girl and her friend sitting by the roadside and took advantage of the poor illumination. They started making lewd comments and jeered at the duo. When the girl's friend objected to their obscenity, a quarrel broke out. "Three of them dismounted from the two-wheelers, and one of them restrained the boy while two others held the girl. Seeing this, two from the group sped away on one of the two-wheelers. Thereafter, one of the three caught hold of the boy while two others took turns to rape her at the same spot," Vadodara SP Rohan Anand said, adding the trio fled around 12:30am. Anand said that the girl and the boy were unable to see the accused properly as it was dark. The area has been cordoned off. Some pieces of the girl's jewellery, as well as gadgets suspected to belong to the accused, were found at the location. TNN

When a huge police force, led by the Baruipur SDPO, reached the area and burst tear gas shells, the mob attacked the officer with brooms and sticks. Twelve policemen were injured. "We will continue our agitation till the accused are punished. We demand action against cops who delayed acting on the complaint. The girl could possibly have been rescued had the cops acted promptly," one of the girl's neighbours, Ganesh Dolui, said. The cops denied the allegations.

Politicians made a beeline to Mahismari. Among them was Joynagar MP Pratima Mandal from the governing TMC. She and her party colleagues faced protesters' ire. The MP also had a heated exchange with BJP's Agnimitra Paul. "Why did cops refuse to act after receiving the complaint?" Paul asked. CPM leaders, too, trooped in.

Protesters clashed with cops a second time when the girl's body was sent to a morgue in Kolkata's Mominpur for post-mortem.

News of 6th october 2024.

It may be pertinent to note that weapons of injury and their training or use should be restrained in the family by the parents. In a news from Pune on october 18th 2024, a 13 year old boy was injured as loaded revolver in a bag went off after fall from cupboard. The boy returned home from the school and opened the cupboard to get some clothes out. The bag containing the revolver was kept on the upper rack. The boy's shoulder brushed against the bag and it fell as he opened the cupboard in his flat at Dhankawadi. The boy Abhay Shirne was taken to hospital. The case was registered against the boy's father under section 125. The bullet pierced the boy's left leg and he was shifted to the hospital. Though the case was registered against his father, his case of offense cannot be denied that he guided his family minors of retention of pistol in the family and he was not conscious that weapon if not handled properly may affect him and the society. The mistake of the parent certainly reflected the child and such values to children are bad in law. The only news item could not solve the problem but there should be a course of action on a regulation of misuse of weapons in presence of minors and law must take its own course to curb this type of careless social evils.

TOI, Oct 18 2024

13-yr-old boy injured as loaded revolver in bag goes off after fall from cupboard

Gitesh Shelke
@timesofindia.com

Pune: A 13-year-old boy sustained a bullet injury to his leg after a loaded revolver kept in a bag in a cupboard, went off when the bag fell as he opened the cupboard in his flat in Dhankawadi around 3.15pm on Tuesday.

The boy, Abhay Shirke, was taken to a nearby hospital for treatment.

Senior inspector Chhagan Kapse of Sahakarnagar police said, "We have impounded the revolver belonging to his father, Nitin Shirke (40), a retired army jawan, who now works as a guard at the bungalow of a state minister in Katraj. Shirke secured the firearm licence from Srinagar during his posting in Jammu & Kashmir while he was in the Army. He also purchased the revolver from there."

"We have registered a case under Section 125 (rash or negligent acts that put human life or personal safety at risk) against the boy's father, who should have kept the firearm unloaded and in a safe place in his house," he said.

"The boy returned home from school and opened the cupboard to get out some clothes. The bag containing the revolver was kept on the upper rack. The boy's shoulder brushed against the bag, and it fell. The gun misfired as soon as the bag landed on the floor," Kapse added.

The bullet pierced the boy's left leg, and he was shifted to the hospital by neighbours. Police said he is now out of danger.

> The boy returned home from school and opened the cupboard to get out some clothes. The bag containing the revolver was kept on the upper rack. The boy's shoulder brushed against the bag, and it fell
>
> **Chhagan Kapse** | SENIOR INSPECTOR, SAHAKARNAGAR POLICE

The above prescription of 24th October 2024 speculates that neither the government is concerned nor the agency working on juvenile delinquency are serious in the matters of juvenile decisions. In appropriate time with appropriate decisions. As per the news item it is clear that removal of two officials of JJB, Pune for grant of bail to a 17 year old son of a builder who killed while driving two software engineers in May 2024 were removed from their positions. The vacancy was not filled up by the appropriate authorities. The publication says that Pune JJB likely to get new members after election. This indicates callousness of the policymakers who did not consider appointments or representation

157

of the officials for award of orders in time in the matter of correction of juvenile delinquency. The certainty of elections and its impact afterwards makes a speculation that appointments are also not of quality so that redressal in juveniles crime can be dealt properly and orders are given in time. But the time is coming when juveniles matter will be a serious offense for future days if not solved through a legislation or proper substitute of authorities in dealing the matter in time.

While discussing the child issue towards education and reformation, parents should have been concious of weapon use not to be copied by the children. The use of children by terrorist for stone pelting and weaponary use has now become the model in the cause of terror activites in our country. The lawmakers are aware of such trends that children are being misused but it cannot be said that only person teaching this values is responsible. In present days, children are very intelligent and can also ask their conscience if they need to be adopted for such type of activities for social disorders. Had there been any juvenile punishment as per the law in India for such type of offense committed by them, their must have been control in juvenile crimes but the law is silent and media and policymakers are active that children are being used. This needs to be checked through laws for children punishment so that guardians will restrict the children not to be guided or misutilised by the others in society. The publication of 18th october as above is evidence which indicates parent carelessness and lack of guidance for their own children.

158

Considering the nature of crimes growing and present days juveniles adopting various methodologies as tools for the crimes, there is necessity of look of reorganizing juvenile justice system in the country with appropriate legal system with reformation and rehabilitation so that they can be a good person in the society. Reformatory school, Hazaribagh containing 300 acres of land, workshops, playgrounds, agriculture farms, remained unattended years together due to closure of the instittution and loss of valuable properties should have been placed on administrators for misuse and wastage of such properties. Nobody came forward to convey their concern. Hazaribagh happens to be a beautiful place where Britishers had established a central jail as well as reformatory school in the sides of the lakes with jungles making stress on builiding of characters of offenders and to feel that they have been placed at distance from family and sent to another family only for their crimes. Unfortunately, that consideration was lost with the closure of the reformatory school. Opening of a residential girls school by the Bihar government and subsequently by Jharkhand government in restriced area was not a justice either to juvenile system in the state or to the girls students who were not given vocational training in such valuable workshops containing machines from foreign countries and other ingredients. The residential girls were only allowed school education therefore the entire infrastructure collapsed. Remodeling of the building in a very low manner entirely changed the architechture of the building and large space inside remained

159

closed and outside was misused. The britishers made boundary walls of heights with stones as a security measure but are decaying and is at a state of collapse. The colony quarter collapsed, farmhouses collapsed, water tanks vanished, sweeper colony demolished, playground remained unused, workshop with costly machines was locked and closed and remained defunct. School materials remained closed. Pilot centers with psychologists then constructed in 60s under a scheme of Bihar government headed by senior psychologist Ram Babu Mishra and junior psychologist Rameshwar Singh Vidhyabhushan set etc. has now turned as media house located near lake no. 3 and 4. This same pilot center was having very useful tools and play material for recreation of juvenile children housed in Patwaris on rental basis. The post of probation officer were abolished. Infrastructure collected with reformatory schools inmates was a model of good correction of juveniles being trained in industrial attending institutes who were employed by different institutions and maintaining their families after release. Photographs of decaying compounds and houses are being placed.

The latest news of ToI (30th October 2024) is a report of Chhattisgarh high court which has dismissed a petition to release a 24 year old who was a juvenile when detained in a POCSO case saying that taking a lenient view in such cases

161

would open flood gates for similarly convicted juveniles which would be highly detrimental to society and may create a law and order situation. The bench of chief justice Ramesh Sinha and justice Vibhudatta Guru upheld the decision of Kondagoan Seshan Court to transfer the convict to a prison for adults as he has crossed the age limit of 21. He was around 17 years old at theh time of offense in 2017. In 2019 he was found guilty of gangrape and POCSO act and sentenced to 20 years imprisonment. The convict had moved high court pleading for release based on positive reformatory progress report after the Seshan court ordered that he be shifted from the shelter for juvenile to prison.

This confirms our position that leniency should not be granted in the act so that child offenders take advantage of law in creating mischief in society which has now also been confirmed by several decisions of the high courts. Therefore the government should now be stripped in adopting law and a model-like reformatory school act.

Decaying night security gumti along with boundary walls deteriorating.

Boundary walls are under collapse.

Boundary walls from distance.

Quarters retained by chief warden Madhusudhan
Mishra. Decaying and collapsing.

163

Leftover damaged quarters.

Abundant agricultural farm (1 out of 4 at Kolghati)

164

Mihir Lal Banerjee unable to trace out earlier
house of Kunjalal Banerjee quarter which
collapsed.
The legislatures, parliamentrians, administrators,
media and social reformers have to give a look
to bad nature of homes of juveniles existing in
the country meet for the reformation. No
accountability of the government in management
of old homes, ragged schools, reformatory
schools in the country as well as then facilitory
existing was not used nor adopted. The JJB only

165

deciding nature of crimes and to decide if the child case is to be dealt by child court or adult court in context of 2015 act will not solve the case. The laws should be in response to a crime law of the country for minors. Therefore, attempt should be to make the rules in proper ways to build up the juvenile's future to join them in civil society. The vocational and industrial training along with the agriculture education, school education should be developed in home institutions. Present day education on pharmacy, nursing, horticulture be made available in the juvenile homes failing which the homes should not be recognized.

The justice system under the umbrella of institutions should also be punitive with reformation and rehabilitation. This should be mandatory mechanism in fulfilment of minors reformation as juveniles. Mere counseling and psychological treatment is not a solution in resolving the crime characters. The offenders should have realisation of misdeeds through appropriate repentance as well as proper capacity of future earning, getting skills, training and education. Poverty, lack of family support, illiteracy may not be the cause in the development of bad conduct as the poor man has also sometimes better conscience than rich. There is a need of check and balance with a good conduct or bad conduct. The society has now to think if they have some responsibility in the matter and should educate the policymakers not to be casual in reshaping the valued life making them as juveniles, to commit crimes. This is not a good step in countries better future and we must feel proud as Indians to contribute

166

good and to reform our generation in proper manner.

Recommendations:

Few suggestions are being placed for adoption as recommendations.

1. The juvenile homes be reformatory schools.
2. The school should contain workshops, schools, agriculture farms etc.
3. Proper dormitory with water and electrical facilities should be made available.
4. The kitchen should be divisible as per groups.
5. Proper kitchen facility must be made.
6. Hospital and doctors within the campus must be regular employees.
7. Proper playground should be created.
8. Recreational stay and facilities be created.
9. The campus should have schools with tenth and plus two systems
10. Proper boundary of the campus be kept to avoid inmates to move outside the campus at their will.
11. The release of inmates after period be made to parents at home by staff of the school.
12. Probation officer, psychologist be provided as routine employee.
13. Educational teachers, chief warden, doctors, foreman must be permanent employee.

167

14. Reform system should be considered on nature of crimes coming up

15. Age of boys and girls for definition as juveniles be the same.

16. Establishment of juvenile boards but not the JJB.

17. Childcare protection be different than juvenile delinquents.

18. Proper infrastructure and staff, state and central government should take burden of salary and maintenance.

19. There should not be categorization of age and crimes.

20. A survey be made of old reformatory schools, ragged schools by the government by a committee for recommendation of practical scheme on reformation of juvenile delinquents along with placement proposal after completion of their tenure. All these facilites was available in the reformatory school, Hazaribagh and might be in reformatory school, Yerwada and Chinglapet, Chennai, Madras.

About the Author

The author has long experience of dealing with students, youths and upgrowing children. He was professor and a Dean of Students Welfare in the university system under Odisha University of Agriculture and Technology. While being educated in Anada High School of Hazaribagh and having scope of realising importance of

Reformatory School in Hazaribagh is very much constrained on present policy of the government which lack reformation and rehabilitation of the juvenile delinquents for their participation in the society. Accordingly, he has tried to collect information of growing crimes of juveniles in the country and has tried to present necessity of reformatory schools for the purpose of juvenile connections. Author has also written books of student agitation namely Quest and Struggle and Odisha Legislation, Agriculture Education, agriculture productions and crops etc.. In preparation of this book Author is happy in participation of granddaughter of Ritisha Dash (12) and Dishita Dash (15) who have helped in preparation of this book.

-Dr. Budhadev Mishra.